the Artful Bride

ROCKPORT

April L. Paffrath and Laura McFadden

the Artful Bride

SIMPLE, HANDMADE WEDDING PROJECTS

ROCKPORT PUBLISHERS

First published in the United States of America by
Rockport Publishers, Inc.
33 Commercial Street
Gloucester, Massachusetts 01930-5089
Telephone: (978) 282-9590
Fax: (978) 283-2742
www.rockpub.com

Library of Congress Cataloging-in-Publication Data
Paffrath, April L.
    The artful bride : simple, handmade wedding projects / April L.
Paffrath and Laura McFadden.
        p.   cm.
    ISBN 1-56496-961-4 (pbk.)
    1. Handicraft. 2. Weddings—Equipment and supplies. 3. Wedding decorations. I. McFadden, Laura. II. Title.
TT149 .P34 2003
    745.594'1—dc21   2002014882

ISBN 1-56496-961-4

10 9 8 7 6 5 4 3 2 1

Design: Laura McFadden Design, Inc.
Cover Image: Bobbie Bush Photography,
www.bobbiebush.com
Photography: Bobbie Bush Photography, www.bobbiebush.com
Illustrations: Pages 46, 47, 49, 76, 77, 80,
84, 85, Mary Newell DePalma
Illustrations: Pages 66, 124, Carolynn DeCillo
All other illustrations and diagrams: Laura McFadden
Project Manager and Copyeditor: Lindsay Stoms
Proofreader: Heather Gurk

Printed in Singapore

Contents

8 Introduction
124 Templates
126 Resources
128 About the Authors
128 Acknowledgments

Correspondence

10

12 THE RIGHT BUTTONS *Invitation Enclosure Envelope*
16 SAY IT WITH FLOWERS *Pansy Envelope Invitation*
18 TIME TO RSVP *Organdy Ribbon Vellum Invitation*
20 ECO-INVITE *Leaf Window Invitation*
22 MATERIAL WORLD *Fabric Invitation*
24 FLOCKING TOGETHER *Origami Announcement*
28 BLOSSOMING THANKS *3D Note Cards*
30 BUDGETING TIME

Gifts & Goodies

32

34 FIELD OF FLOWERS *Photo Pebble Resin Frame*
35 WHEN THE PARTY'S OVER ALBUM *Mini Portfolio of Party Pictures*
42 JORDAN BOMBONIÈRE *Tulle Bundles with Style*
44 FLOWER POWER JEWELRY *Beaded Ring, Necklace, and Bracelet*
50 MOONING OVER MEMORIES *Paper and Moonstone Frame*
54 GUEST SURVIVAL KIT *Hotel Room Goodies*
56 THE BEAT GOES ON *Music CD*
58 CUPPA QUIET *Paint-Your-Own-Pottery Tea Kit*
60 KNICKERS WITH A TWIST *Personalized Panties for Your Pals*
64 MAYBE, BABY! *Retro Ball Bearing Toy*
67 ADAPTING STYLE

Ceremony Details

70   CUSHION OF LOVE *Ring Bearer's Pillow*

74   PRACTICAL PRINCESS-WEAR *Subtle Tiara*

78   TWINKLE TOES *Shoe Decorations*

82   DYNAMIC COLLIER *Metal and Bead Choker*

86   GUIDED BY ANCESTORS

Reception & Decor

90   HUNKA BURNIN' LOVE *Photo Votive*

92   THE TIES THAT BIND *Japanese-Style Photo Album*

98   ZEN CENTERPIECE *Sleek Bamboo Garden*

100   A GARDEN OF ONE'S OWN *Zen Rock Garden*

102   TOYING WITH GUESTS *Wind-up Name Cards*

106   TIERS OF JOY *Wedding Cake Card Box*

110   CHAPEL OF LOVE *Sacred Table Topper*

114   STICKY GUEST BOOK *iZone Booklet for Each Table*

116   KIDDIE CONFECTIONS *Lollipop Bouquet*

118   WHERE DO I SIT? *Miniature Seat Assignments*

120   MINI FRAME TO GO *Place Card Frame in Organdy Sack*

122   CRAFTY WAYS OF FINDING HELP

Introduction

A wedding is a romantic and special event for a couple. It is the culmination of a lot of planning—and a party you host for your family and friends. Creative and modern couples are often confronted with the option of warming over the traditional elements that find a home in everyone else's weddings. But we know you have your own sense of style. In everyday life, you expertly straddle social convention and your own personal flair. (For those who don't, there is Emily Post.) When it comes to weddings, however, women are confronted with demands from all sides, and a history that attempts to live up to Queen Victoria's legacy. (She started the white dress trend, after all.)

Clearly, not everyone gets married in Victoria and Albert style—or in Elvis' chapel of love. Most people fall somewhere in between. We've come up with ideas for the savvy middle group, with an occasional homage to either end of the spectrum. This book will provide ideas to help you create a wedding that has a real personality—your own.

photo by Bobbie Bush

A wedding has style only when it is infused with your ideas and humor. When you invite people to a wedding, you are throwing a great celebration for the people closest to you—the people who know you best. This is no time to cling to tired-out traditions or overdone details. Will the party be more fun if you add contrived elements to every aspect? Probably not—so leave the napkins alone.

The people you invite to your wedding know your sense of humor, your charm, and even your kooky taste in music. Don't be tempted to bury those qualities under layers of standard wedding elements. Create your own invitations, cards, favors, tiaras, and centerpieces. Consider how to adapt each item to your style and have a blast with it. Handmade wedding elements are fun to make, they give you greater control over the feel of your wedding, and they even provide you with some quality downtime during the preparation for the big day.

Correspondence

Correspondence is the first and last way you involve guests in your wedding. Your friends and family may not have even heard the marital buzz when invitations arrive in their mailboxes. And weeks later they are doubtless still talking about the amazing time they had celebrating when they receive a thank-you in the mail.

Invitations are the first clue guests have about what kind of a party you two are hosting. And, although strict adherents to etiquette bibles may shriek in horror, you can pick whatever you want to say and how to say it. Even Emily Post now agrees that an invitation does not have to be worded in the traditional manner. The year does not have to be spelled out and the "honour" of someone's presence can be requested in just about any way that reflects your personality. But, as an official invitation, it must include the crucial information: who, what, where, and when. Beyond that, the door is wide open to make the invitation memorable for more than fine engraving. Often the smallest weddings are announced with excited phone calls rather than a letterpress run of fifteen, so don't feel obligated to walk in other people's footsteps. In this chapter, we've included some examples that show how invitations can reflect different styles, using similar techniques. We also share some ways of packaging the invitation and essential information.

Thank-you notes are always in order. The fact that friends and family celebrated with you whole-heartedly is, in itself, a wonderful gift worthy of great thanks. That's not even to mention the assorted crystal, towels, paintings, vases, and toasters that may accompany your guests' earnest and personal well-wishes. Our thank-you ideas provide an elegant canvas for your note. As for writing the cards themselves, you and your sweetie should strive to stand out a little. It is very important to thank people for any gifts they have given you, but it is even more important to tell them what their presence meant to you. Go on, you can do it.

The Right Buttons

We can be pretty sure we're holding a wedding invitation in our hands when we open an envelope and find another tucked inside. Back in the days when footmen hand-delivered invitations of all sorts, the exterior envelope got messy from all the handling, while the interior enclosure stayed pristine. Now the mail carriers take care of the delivery, but the process is none the cleaner. An interior envelope remains the signal that we are opening something important. One way to make the enclosure envelope stand out and grab some attention is to make it feel and seal differently than other beautiful, traditional versions.

This two-toned vellum envelope looks elegant with its overlapping sheer colors and deckled edging. It is made whimsical and sweet by the button mechanism and the tiny photos of the two of you embedded in either button. To close the envelope, people tie the two of you together by winding a thread around the buttons. The sheer vellum invitation rests inside the flaps.

1. Fold the piece of 8 ½" x 11" (21.6 cm x 27.9 cm) pink vellum in half, short sides together. Score the fold with a bone folder to make the edge crisp. Cut the long side down to 6" (15.2 cm) so that, folded, the paper measures 4 ¼" x 6" (10.8 cm x 15.2 cm).

2. Repeat the same process with the green vellum.

3. Lay folded pink vellum on work surface so that folded edge is on your right. Spray adhesive on the back of the pink vellum, the side that is touching the work surface. (Spray the adhesive in a separate, well-ventilated area. The glue will stick to everything on your work area otherwise.)

TIP *If you want to use 2-hole or 4-hole buttons instead of shank buttons, simply sew the buttons on first and then inset the photos.*

MATERIALS

8 ½" × 11" (21.6 cm × 27.9 cm) sheets of pink and green vellum

4 ¾" × 6 ½" (12.1 cm × 16.5 cm) pink vellum envelopes

8 ½" × 11" (21.6 cm × 27.9 cm) sheets of white vellum for laser or inkjet printers

Personal computer

Photocopier or scanner and printer

Your favorite computer layout software

Pink embroidery thread

¾" (1.9 cm)-wide shank buttons with a raised edge (that creates an inset for photos)

Deckled-edge decorative scissors

Bone folder

Craft knife

Scissors

Photos of you and your partner

Spray adhesive

Pencil

Template to match size of button inset

Pink sewing thread

Sewing needle

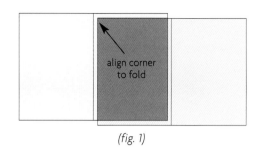

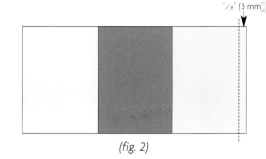

⅛" (3 mm)

(fig. 1)   *(fig. 2)*

4. Open up the green vellum sheet, like a book, and lay it flat. Adhere the sprayed side of the pink vellum to the green vellum this way: align the left edge of the sprayed panel with the fold line of the green vellum *(see fig. 1)*. The right edge of the green vellum should line up with the fold line of the pink vellum. Smooth out any bumps or bubbles with the bone folder.

5. Use a craft knife to cut another ⅛" (3 mm) from the free flap of the pink vellum *(see fig. 2)*.

6. Fold in the pink flap, then overlap with the free flap of the green. Score the folds with the bone folder to help the piece lay flat.

7. Open out the green vellum front cover flap. Measure and cut the green flap in half so it measures 2⅛" wide x 6" high (5.4 cm x 15.2 cm) as shown in *fig. 3*.

8. With a pencil, mark the center of the free edge of the green vellum *(see fig. 4)*. Make two other marks on the top and bottom of the flap, ½" (1.3 cm) in from folded edges.

9. Using a pencil and ruler, connect the top and bottom marks to the center mark, forming a pointed flap for the envelope.

10. With the decorative scissors, cut along pencil lines.

11. Reduce the photos to fit inside the buttons. You can do this at home with a scanner and printer, or you can take them to a copy center and have several made at once. Make sure you take a button with you to double-check the size. Do some experimenting at home with a plain piece of paper to make sure you get the correct size circles to nest into the buttons. Use a circle guide and a little trial-and-error. Ours worked well with a ⁵⁄₁₆" (8 mm) circle guide, but different buttons may vary.

12. Place a circle guide over the photos and draw a pencil line around the inside of the hole.

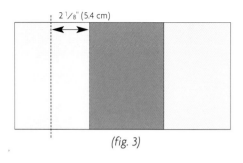

2 ⅛" (5.4 cm)

(fig. 3)

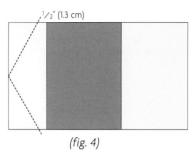

½" (1.3 cm)

(fig. 4)

13. Cut out photos with scissors and spray mount backs of photos. Inset photos into center of buttons.

14. Sew one button onto the green flap, about ½" (1.3 cm) in from point. Sew another button onto pink side, about ½" (1.3 cm) to the right of closed pointed flap.

15. Measure an 11" (27.9 cm) long strand of the pink embroidery thread and cut. Wrap around buttons.

TO MAKE THE INVITATION

1. Create a new document, 4⅛" x 6" (10.5 cm x 15.2 cm) in MS Word or your layout program.

2. Pick the font. We used Bernhard Tango 15 point.

3. Type your invitation and center the text.

4. Print invitation onto 8½" x 11" (21.6 cm x 27.9 cm) white vellum.

5. Cut out the invitation with craft knife and reopen button closure envelope. Place the invitation inside, close the envelope, and rewrap thread.

VARIATION *If you don't want to use photographs of yourselves in the button centers, try a monogrammed approach by using buttons with each of your initials on them.*

Say It with Flowers

MATERIALS

8 ½" × 11"
(21.6 cm × 27.9 cm)
white vellum
for laser or
inkjet printers

Printer

Personal computer

Your favorite
computer layout
software

Pencil

Metal ruler

Drafting triangle

Craft knife

Hole punch

5 ¼" (13.3 cm)
square yellow
petal envelopes

Yellow and
white swirl paper

³⁄₈" (1 cm)
light purple ribbon,
7" (17.8 cm)
per invitation

Scissors

Pansy stickers

Flowers deservedly have a prominent place in many weddings, because of their beauty and vitality. What better qualities to exalt on this occasion? This invitation is simple decorative paper packaged in a special envelope. The petal style of the envelope and the light yellow and purple colors of the materials make the entire invitation very springy. Seal it with a pansy sticker in the same color range.

1. With your favorite computer layout software, create your 4 ³⁄₈" (11.1 cm) square invitation. Print onto 8 ½" x 11" (21.6 cm x 27.9 cm) vellum. Trim to size.

2. Measure and cut out a 5" (12.7 cm) square of the yellow and white swirl paper.

3. Place vellum on top of swirl paper and make two tick marks with your pencil, ½" (1.3 cm) from the top edge and 2 ¼" (5.7 cm) from both the left and right edges of the layered sheets.

4. Punch holes in marked areas. Tie the two sheets of paper together by knotting a 7" (17.8 cm) piece of light purple ribbon through the holes. Trim ends on a diagonal.

5. Place in petal envelope and seal envelope with a pansy sticker.

VARIATION *Place two faux wedding bands in the middle of the knot of purple ribbon, leaving enough space under the rings so the invitation wording is not covered up.*

PLEASE COME JOIN US
IN THE CELEBRATION OF
OUR WEDDING
KIM FURNALD
&
TIM GRAY
JUNE 8, 2003
1 P.M.
HILLISTON HISTORICAL SOCIETY
128 OLD CAMBRIDGE ROAD
HILLISTON, MA
RECEPTION TO FOLLOW

Time to RSVP

An invitation is a unique piece of mail. Layered materials give recipients plenty to experience. It lets them know that the occasion is special and attention-worthy. This invitation combines several decorative papers that open like a triptych to reveal a skeleton leaf and a sheer vellum invitation. The texture of the varied materials invokes the feeling you and your spouse-to-be are trying to create, whether it's sleek, folksy, ethereal, or something completely different. Spend some time perusing the paper choices until you find a combination that best represents your style.

1. With your favorite computer layout software, create your 3 ½" x 5 ¼" (8.9 cm x 13.3 cm) invitation. Print onto 8 ½" x 11" (21.6 cm x 27.9 cm) vellum. Trim to size.

2. Measure and cut out an 8 ½" wide x 6" (21.6 cm x 15.2 cm) piece of cream paper and decorative paper. Spray mount two sides together, decorative sides facing out.

3. Place cream side facing up. Measure and mark a vertical line with a pencil, 2 ¼" (5.7 cm) in on left and right sides of wide part of paper. Fold paper in on pencil lines with a bone folder. Erase pencil lines.

4. Open up cover and place vellum invitation inside, adhering it to the interior cream side of the cover with photo corners.

5. Place leaf over invitation and fold cover shut.

6. Cut a 25" (63.5 cm) length of ribbon and tie around outside with a bow.

TIP *When you select your paper, keep in mind the invitation size; a small pattern may have more impact than large, dynamic graphics.*

MATERIALS

8 ½" × 11" (21.6 cm × 27.9 cm) white vellum for laser or inkjet printers

Printer

Personal computer

Your favorite computer layout software

Pencil

Metal ruler

Drafting triangle

Craft knife

Bone folder

White eraser

4 ½" × 6 ¼" (11.4 cm × 15.9 cm) cream envelopes

Matching cream paper

Decorative paper

Tan skeleton leaves

Spray adhesive

Photo corners

1" (2.5 cm) coordinating organdy or organza ribbon

Eco-Invite

MATERIALS

8 ½" × 11"
(21.6 cm × 27.9 cm)
white vellum for
laser or inkjet printers

Printer

Personal computer

Your favorite computer
layout software

Pencil

Metal ruler

Drafting triangle

Craft knife

5 ¼" (13.3 cm)
square tan petal
envelopes

Green and tan
variegated
decorative paper

Green leaf
decorative paper

Small green
leaf skeletons

Spray adhesive

There are so many reasons to love this woodsy invitation. You don't have to be a hiker, an ecologist, or a weekend garden-partier, but you do have to like amazing forest tones and tree imagery. If you are getting married outdoors, this invitation is a natural (in so many ways).

If natural, recycled papers are important to you, you're in luck with this project. Some of the most popular natural options are the patterns and styles that best create this look.

1. With your favorite computer layout software, create your 10" wide x 5" high (25.4 cm x 12.7 cm) invitation. Design the text to fit on 5" x 5" (12.7 cm x 12.7 cm) area on the right side of the document. Print onto 8 ½" x 11" (21.6 cm x 27.9 cm) vellum. Trim to size.

2. Measure and cut out a 10" x 5" (25.4 cm x 12.7 cm) piece of both the leaf paper and variegated paper. Spray mount two sides together, decorative sides facing out.

3. Place variegated side facing up. Measure and cut a 1 ½" x 2" (3.8 cm x 5.1 cm) window, 1 ¾" (4.4 cm) from the right edge and 1 ½" (3.8 cm) from the top edge of the paper.

4. Flip the paper over so the leafy side is facing up. Spray the leafy side of paper with spray adhesive. Adhere vellum invitation to leafy side of paper. Make sure the invitation words are to the right of the window and do not overlap the opening. Fold invitation in half so it measures 5" (12.7 cm) square.

5. Close the invitation. Spray the back of the skeleton leaf with adhesive and place in center of window.

VARIATION *You don't have to use two different decorative papers. You can skip the inside paper, if you like the look of the "wrong" side of the main paper. The process will be simpler, but the look may not be as finished as with two designs.*

We're getting hitched!
Our joy will be more complete
if you celebrate with us.
Nimali Jacobson
&
Hermes Fernands
Saturday, October 6, 2003
4 p.m.
St. Thomas Church
New York, New York

Material World

The vibrant color and lush silver on this invitation recall a history of marking celebrations with decadent materials and intricate handiwork. Fabrics add dynamic colors and patterns, as well as a textural layer, to your invitation. The project is simple, but the combination of textures makes it feel intricate.

1. With your favorite computer layout software, create your 3 ½" x 5 ½" (8.9 cm x 14 cm) invitation. Print onto 8 ½" x 11" (21.6 cm x 27.9 cm) vellum. Trim to size.

2. Measure and cut out a 4" x 6" (10.2 cm x 15.2 cm) piece of corrugated paper. Center vellum on top of corrugated paper and place a tick mark with your pencil ¾" (1.9 cm) from top and 2" (5.1 cm) from the left (this should be dead center, left to right). Make a hole through the two layers with a hole punch.

3. Drop your eyelet grommet through the hole so decorative side of grommet faces front of the invitation. Place invitation layers face down and place eyelet setting tool through back of hole. Hit punch with a hammer so edges of eyelet flange outward. Once edges have flanged, hit back of eyelet again until edges flatten.

4. To make cover: Measure and cut out a 10" wide x 6" (25.4 cm x 15.2 cm) piece of material gift wrap. Lay flat horizontally, wrong side up. Measure in 3" (7.6 cm) from the sides on both sides and draw a pencil line to mark. Fold inward on pencil line and score edges with a bone folder.

5. On the left flap, place a tick mark with your pencil ¼" (6.4 mm) in from flap edge and 3" (7.6 cm) from the top. Make a hole with a hole punch.

6. Place the grommet through the hole, decorative side out. Finish grommet as in step three.

7. Place finished invitation inside material sleeve and tie with a tassel. The tassel will not fit through the eyelet hole so follow this procedure: Push a small loop of tassel cord through the back of the eyelet, and out through the front of the cover flap. Make a loop in other tie end and tie the two loops in a bow.

VARIATION *This format can be used for more than invitations. Try a fabric treatment for a reception dinner menu or a program of events. Guests unwrap the tassel tie to see what is written inside.*

MATERIALS

8 ½" × 11" (21.6 cm × 27.9 cm) white vellum for laser or inkjet printers

Printer

Personal computer

Your favorite computer layout software

Wavy, silver corrugated paper

Pencil

Metal ruler

Drafting triangle

Craft knife

3 mm eyelet grommets

Hole punch

Eyelet setting tool

Hammer

Stiff Indian material gift wrap (decorative paper can be substituted)

Bone folder

Tassels with strings

Flocking Together

ORIGAMI ANNOUNCEMENT

MATERIALS

Origami
paper squares

1/4" (6.4 mm)
wide satin ribbon

Thread that
matches the
ribbon color

Sewing needle

Personal
computer

Printer

Your favorite
computer
layout software

Scissors

Envelope

Decorative
straw

You want a tradional announcement? You know where Crane's is located, friends. There's nothing wrong with that at all—it's one of our favorite stationers. But what about creative and amusing, or even a little out of the ordinary? That you're going to have to do yourself, with no help from the kings of kid-finish paper.

Finding a new type of announcement can be a little daunting. We relied on a history of amazing, but easy, origami to create a mailable vignette to herald the news. Three-dimensional items can be tricky to send through the postal service, so it helps to keep things small and basic. We thought a bird of a simple feather would travel well.

1. With your favorite computer layout software, create a box 2 1/8" wide x 2 1/4" high (5.4 cm x 5.7 cm). Type your announcement text in the box, using your favorite typeface.

2. Print out as many copies as announcements to send. Cut out each printout.

3. Roll each piece of paper and tie with a 3" (7.6 cm) piece of ribbon.

4. Lay the square of origami paper, decorative side up. Fold the paper in half once, point to point. Unfold, leaving a crease down the middle *(see fig. 1)*.

5. Flip the paper over. Fold the left and right corners to the middle crease, aligning the paper edges along the crease *(see fig. 2)*.

6. Fold the entire figure in half along the original crease. Fold the tip of the paper to the front, then to the back. Then unfold leaving a crease *(see fig. 3)*.

VARIATION *Use two pieces of origami paper for a unique contrast. Place wrong sides together, use spray mount to hold them together if needed. The contrasting pattern will show on the bird's tail.*

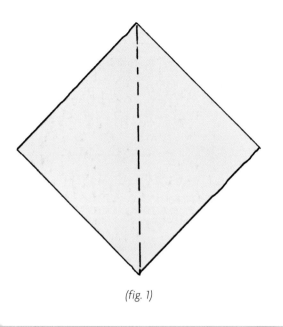

(fig. 1)

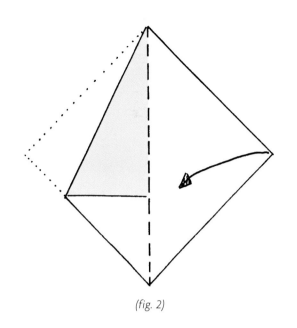

(fig. 2)

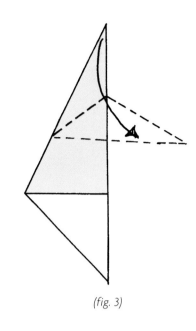

(fig. 3)

7. Invert the fold along the point, using the creases from step six. The result should look a little like a rabbit ear *(see fig. 4)*.

8. Follow the same strategy further up the point. Fold to the front, then fold to the back, then unfold, leaving a crease *(see fig. 5)*.

9. Repeat the same inversion further up the point to form the head of the bird *(see fig. 6)*.

10. Lay the bird flat and fold up the top layer of the body to meet with the "back." Flip over and repeat on the other side *(see fig. 7)*.

11. With the needle and thread, attach the ribbon-tied scroll to the beak of the bird. Double the thread so it will not break in transit.

12. Fold the bird flat, and package in an envelope with some decorative straw.

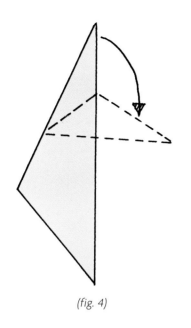

(fig. 4)

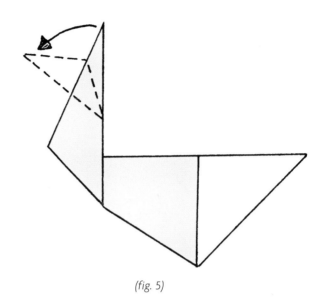

(fig. 5)

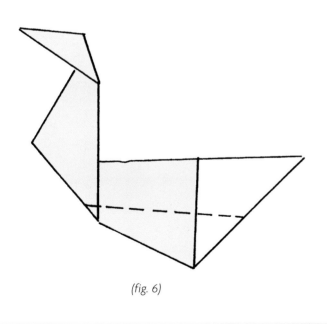

(fig. 6)

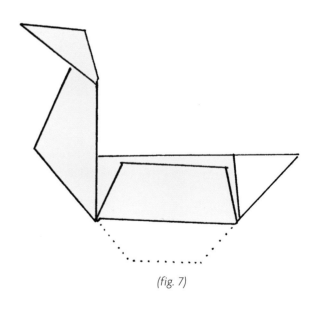

(fig. 7)

Blossoming Thanks

3D NOTE CARDS

MATERIALS

Small photo pebbles

Personal computer and color printer or photocopier

Plain white paper

Adhesive paper flowers and stems

Plain 5 5/16" × 3 13/16" (13.5 cm × 9.7 cm) note cards

8 1/2" × 11" (21.6 cm × 27.9 cm) vellum paper

Craft knife

Decorative-edge scissors

4" × 5" (10.2 cm × 12.7 cm) envelopes

PVA glue

Spray mount adhesive

Inexpensive paintbrush

Bone folder

Template from page 124

Elaborate-looking thank-you notes don't necessarily take forever to make. Nor do you have to buy them in packs of ten. These flower cards are a matter of simple assembly-line construction — but their effect is anything but plain. Using photo pebbles, your thanks are magnified and stand out from the usual notes available.

When your hand is cramping after writing what feels like the five thousandth card, prevent your tuckered hand from giving the wrong impression. The liquid ink used in roller ball and fountain pens will make your handwriting appear smoother than a ballpoint pen, which shows every shake. If you're unfamiliar with fountain pens, practice writing your to-do lists with them. Think smooth.

1. Color copy the template from page 124 or print "thanks" logos onto plain white paper. You can also create your own design using your favorite computer layout software or handwrite them with permanent ink.

2. With a paintbrush, spread a thin layer of PVA on the flat surface of the photo pebble and center over the "thanks" image. To ensure the image doesn't run, do not move the photo pebble once you've put it in place. Wait for the glue to set (about 10 minutes).

3. Cut out the paper around the pebble with a craft knife, removing extraneous paper.

4. Spray mount colored vellum onto the note card and smooth out any bubbles with the bone folder. Fold paper in half along the natural fold of the note card. Score the fold with the bone folder.

5. Trim note card and paper with the decorative-edged scissors.

6. Adhere paper flower and stem to the center of the card.

7. Glue the pebble to the center of the flower.

TIP *If you are creating your own "thanks" images, experiment with the photo pebble to make sure the finished product is legible—the photo pebble magnifies the word and can cut off the image edges if the letters are too large.*

Budgeting Time

Photographer/Artist: Monica Lau, Getty Images

We cannot say this enough: Start early. More importantly: Finish early. Plenty of things can be frustrating when planning a wedding, but very little has to be. Do everything you can to eliminate the difficulties that come with running out of time. That frustration is the main reason many people hire consultants to do everything for them, figuring that it's better to lose money than to lose your cool. But, you may not need to decide between the two, if you keep time in mind. Granted, no amount of help we or anyone else offer can eliminate chilly feet or a lifetime of communication difficulties with your mother. If these are problems you've got, find a consultant and a stack of post-its and mark your favorite pages of this book for him or her so you can focus on other things.

SET YOUR OWN EXPECTATIONS

If you expect everything to run smoothly and turn out perfectly, chances are you won't believe anyone who warns you about being disappointed. If you set unrealistic expectations for yourself, you will be agitated in trying to achieve them, and your chances of having fun diminish greatly. Who wants that? On the other hand, don't believe anyone who says you must get stressed out and reach a breaking point—that's absolute baloney! If you feel unstressed, look at it as a blessing and enjoy the time. It's good to feel satisfied with the plans you've made and the work you've done. Forcing yourself to stress about it will not make your wedding more charming, but it will have an adverse effect on you. It's better to have great memories of your wedding *and* the time leading up to it.

The first step to getting things done on time and done well is to acknowledge that there are intermediate points between perfection and failure. A project that looks beautiful but isn't devoid of flaws is not a failure, it's handmade. Allow yourself to capture the spirit of your relationship, without getting bogged down by perfection anxiety.

TRY PROJECTS OUT

You'll have a greater success with projects if you try them out well in advance. Try out all the projects you are contemplating. Use the ones that turn out best and leave the less-than-gorgeous ones behind. You're committing to a person, not a style of photo frame.

KNOW WHEN TO LET THINGS GO

Most people hire help of some sort for their wedding. Whether it's a florist, a caterer, a restaurant, or judge, choose the people or organizations carefully so you can feel confident about their abilities. The more at ease you are with those providing a service, the more removed you can be from the minutiae. You and your fiancé should convey to everyone involved your desires for each element of the day. Then decide what amount of deviation from your ideal you are willing to accept. Elements you don't want to change will require closer managing. Likewise, if you are unsure about anyone's abilities, you will have to spend more time and energy supervising. If you can handle giving talented people some freedom, it is the best situation to hire people who do a fantastic job and to give them the space to do it.

Sometimes quality relates to budget—but not always. You will have to find the right balance for you. If you are short on time, it can be much better to spend a little more for a super florist than to waste valuable hours going over a plan time and again—or worse, dealing with a floral "catastrophe" on your wedding day.

Letting capable people fully control their roles allows you time to devote as you choose. Perhaps that allows you to arrive at your wedding unfrazzled. Or maybe it frees up enough time for you to leisurely make place cards (see pages 102, 118, 120), mini photo albums (see page 38), and decorative photo frames (see pages 34, 50, 120) for all your guests. ✳

Gifts & Goodies

The gifts and goodies that guests and attendants receive are more than mere presents. They are mementos. Although people will appreciate and enjoy the decorations, the food, and the touching elements that you have folded into your wedding, items that guests take with them are tangible reminders of the day's events. It makes sense, then, to imbue them with the same style, humor, and elegance that shape your wedding and your relationships.

In this chapter, we include gifts that can go to shower guests, attendants, or wedding guests. Favors and gifts don't have to be elaborate or expensive, but they should be thoughtful and indicative of the connection between you and the recipients.

Sometimes brides are ambushed with a surprise wedding shower and therefore have nothing to do with the favors. But many women have significant influence over the style and the favors given.

Most gifts in this section are suitable for everyone. Some gifts, though, are best suited for specific people. Whether your wedding will be a small affair or an event covered in *Town and Country*, your tight group of friends helps you along the way. They assist you in deciding between heels or flats, provide distraction when your mother gets too taxing (it's not her fault), fête your future at your shower, and stand up in fancy outfits during the ceremony. These comrades are the only worthy recipients of "Knickers with a Twist" (see page 60), whereas every wedding or shower guest can enjoy the retro ball bearing game (see page 64).

Deciding which gifts to give out is a fun but difficult task. Consider the complexity of the project and the time involvement. The "Field of Flowers" frame (see page 34) is more complex than the "Mooning Over Memories" frame (see page 50), and is therefore much easier to make for a smaller group of people. If you take into account the time you have available, the intricacy of the project, and the recipients, you are sure to delight guests with tokens that remind them of the wonderful time you have had together.

Field of Flowers

PHOTO PEBBLE RESIN FRAME

Resin starts as a rather toxic liquid (Use it outside and keep it away from children and pregnant women, please!), and solidifies into a unique, rock-hard transparent material. Here, glass pebbles are set into a sea of resin, making a weighty and sculptural photo frame. The glass pebbles magnify the words and images beneath them. We pasted flower images under most of the pebbles. Beneath a few others, we pasted words, the names of the bride and groom, and the wedding date in coordinating colors.

1. Take out the glass and backing of the picture frame. Prime the wood with the white primer. Let dry.

2. With your favorite computer layout software, make a document and import your favorite flower photos. Reduce the images until they look like they will fit under each photo pebble. Duplicate the flower images until you have at least seventy. To test the size, print out a low-quality version of the images and place a few different glass pebbles on them, checking that the image is recognizable and doesn't need to be reduced further. The pebbles vary in size, so try several.

3. Find a typeface suitable to your taste and set some text in a size that will fit under the pebbles. Some ideas for words: the couple's names, the wedding date, and romantic words like "love" and "joy." These can be placed in the same document with the flower images.

VARIATION *Keen on the unique frame, but not much of a floral person? Go for modern graphics like bulls-eye patterns in repeating colors, or plain fields of three different colors.*

MATERIALS

5" × 7" (12.7 cm × 17.8 cm) unpainted wood picture frame with 1 1/2" (3.8 cm) wide border

At least seventy photo pebbles

Personal computer

Glossy photo paper that works for laser or inkjet printers

Color printer

Your favorite computer layout software

Stock CD of images of flowers (also available on Photodisc.com)

PVA glue

16 oz. (473 ml) box Envirotex Lite epoxy (resin)

Small paper bowl

Inexpensive 1/2" (1.3 cm) wide paint brush

White or gray tile grout

Craft knife

White primer

White or ivory semigloss interior latex paint

Masking tape

Two packages white polymer clay

Rolling pin

Hairdryer

7" × 9" (17.8 cm × 22.9 cm) or larger cardboard gift box

Goggles and industrial duty rubber gloves

4. Print the document on glossy photo paper. Print enough copies of the document to get the quantity you need for the pebbles. Wait about 5 minutes for the ink to dry.

5. Pour some PVA glue into a paper bowl. Using a paintbrush, paint a small amount of glue evenly onto the back of a pebble and adhere pebble to flower image or word. To avoid smearing the ink, do not wiggle the pebble once it is on the printout. Repeat this process until all of the pebbles have been placed over a flower or word. Let glue set for about 15 minutes.

6. Use the craft knife to cut out the paper around each pebble. Keep the blade as close to the pebble as possible.

7. Arrange all the pebbles on the frame until you get the look and feel you like. We centered the couple's names and the date on the bottom of the frame. Glue the pebbles into place one by one with PVA glue. Let the pebbles dry in place for 2 hours.

8. Run masking tape around the exterior and interior of the frame.

9. Roll out a 7 ½" x 20" (19.1 cm x 50.8 cm) slab of polymer clay. Cut lengthwise into eight strips 2 ½" (6.4 cm) wide. Press the strips of clay around the exterior and interior walls of the frame, forming a clay wall around the interior and exterior, bringing height of clay up to the height of the pebbles.

10. Place frame in cardboard box.

11. Bring project outdoors or to an area with excellent cross-ventilation. **Important: Please wear industrial gloves and goggles.** The resin is highly toxic. Make sure you read the resin package for all instructions, ingredients, and safety guidelines. Follow package directions. Pour the resin into a plastic cup and stir well. Then pour resin into frame, halfway up the pebble height, and let it set for 5 minutes.

12. Use a hairdryer to get all the air bubbles out of the resin. Let resin set for 24 hours.

13. Remove clay walls, then the masking tape. Paint the sides of the frame with one or two coats of the white or ivory paint and let dry. Replace glass, put your favorite photo in, and pop the backing in place.

TIP *If you don't have digital images of flowers, you can cut them out of catalogs or magazines. Try to find images that are similar to each other in style. You can multiply the images by making color photocopies of your favorites.*

When the Party's Over Album

No doubt, your nuptial festivities will rage on into the night. (Here's to that!) Still, at some point, people have to go home — or out for breakfast. When the party's over, keep the action fresh in people's minds with a little photographic help. Instead of making everyone wait for a peek at your encyclopedia-size wedding album (whenever it gets finished), send everyone his or her own miniature album. You can customize each one, so your college housemate receives a photo of himself raising a glass with your cousin June.

1. Cut bristol board to measure 28" x 5" (71.1 cm x 12.7 cm). Fold in half, so the folded product measures 14" x 5" (35.6 cm x 12.7 cm). Score the fold by running a bone folder along it, making it crisp and straight.

2. Unfold the paper. Fold both paper edges inward to meet the center fold. Score the new folds with the bone folder (see fig. 1).

3. Unfold the new folds and cut ½" (1.3 cm) off both edges. These will be the inside flaps of the photo booklet.

4. Refold the booklet. On the front cover, connect the opposing corners, making two pencil lines that form a big "X." The intersection point is the center of the cover (see fig. 2).

5. Measure out 1" (2.5 cm) from the center point in all directions (top, bottom, right, and left) and mark out the 2" (5.1 cm) square in the middle of the cover (see fig. 3).

6. Cut out the square with a craft knife and ruler. Use a triangle to help keep the cut lines squared.

7. Measure and cut a 30" x 7" (76.2 cm x 17.8 cm) piece of decorative paper.

8. Brush a thin layer of PVA glue on the paper.

TIP *Kolo mass produces this type of album. You could simply paste the decorative paper onto the cover and add the grommets and your own decorative ribbon.*

MATERIALS

One sheet colored bristol board or card stock weight paper, at least 30" × 7" (76.2 cm × 17.8 cm)

One 20" × 30" (50.8 cm × 76.2 cm) sheet cream-colored card stock

One sheet decorative paper (hand block printed or wallpaper)

6 ⅛" (15.6 cm) colored eyelet grommets

1 yard (.9 m) organdy or organza ribbon in coordinating color

One package photo corners

Bone folder

Hammer

Eyelet setting tool

Hole punch

PVA glue

Inexpensive paintbrush

Craft knife

Metal ruler

Sharp pencil

One thumb tack

Drafting triangle

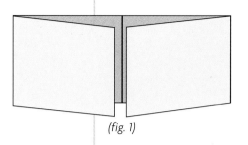
(fig. 1)

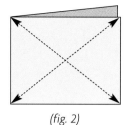
(fig. 2)

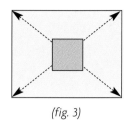
(fig. 3)

9. Flatten out the bristol board cover and place in the center of the paper.

10. Smooth out any bumps in the paper with the bone folder. Let the glue dry approximately ½ hour.

11. Using a craft knife, trim decorative paper down to the size of the bristol board.

12. Place the decorative side down on a cutting surface. Cut two diagonals in the square picture window—upper left corner to lower right, and upper right to lower left.

13. Fold back the newly created triangles, score with bone folder and glue to the non-decorative side *(see fig. 4)*.

14. Make the sheets and endpapers of the book by cutting out three 14" x 5" wide (35. 6 cm x 12.7 cm) rectangles of the cream bristol board.

15. Fold each sheet in half and score with bone folder.

16. Unfold the sheets and stack them. Align the sheets and trim off any excess with the craft knife. Place the sheets into the cover.

17. Break two staples from the pack. Do not staple the book with a stapler.

18. Make a small pencil mark on the outside spine of the cover, ¾" (1.9 cm) from the top and bottom edge. Measure the width of the staple span and make a pencil mark that distance away from both pencil marks.

19. Using your tack, make a hole at each pencil mark, pushing through all four layers. Take care to keep the papers aligned so the hole passes through the fold line in each of the sheets.

20. Center a favorite picture in the inside front cover, so it shows through the photo window. Hold it in place with a little PVA glue or a small piece of drafting tape.

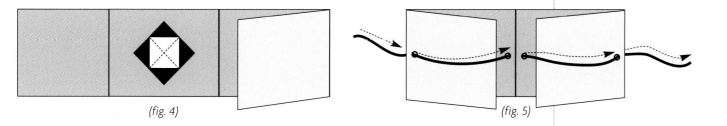

(fig. 4)   (fig. 5)

21. Brush the inside covers with PVA glue and press the first and last pages onto the inside covers, forming the endpapers. Smooth out any bumps with the bone folder. Take care not to press very hard on the picture window.

22. Place the staples through the holes and pinch the staples shut on the center spread by bearing down on staples with a screwdriver.

23. Make a tick mark 2 ½" (6.4 cm) from the bottom edge and ¼" (6.4 mm) in from the spine on front cover. Make another tick mark 2 ½" (6.4 cm) from the bottom edge and ¼" (6.4 mm) in from right edge on cover. Flip book over and do the same on the back.

24. Using hole punch, make a hole in center of all of the tick marked areas. Then open out front and back flaps.

25. Take an eyelet grommet and place the right side through the front hole. Flip book non-decorative side down and place eyelet setting tool through into the back of the grommet. Hit the tool with a hammer until the grommet begins to flange out to the sides of the hole.

26. Repeat this process through all of the holes, keeping grommets' right sides showing on the decorative side of the cover.

27. Close flaps and run ribbon through grommets as follows: Feed ribbon through right front grommet straight into left inside front cover flap grommet. Run ribbon over right inside front flap out through the front spine grommet. Wrap the ribbon around outside spine. Pull through back right spine grommet, run over the inside back flap and out through the right inside back cover flap grommet, and out through the back cover grommet. Trim edges of ribbon evenly *(see fig. 5)*.

28. Using photo corners, place your favorite wedding photos into book and give to family and friends.

Jordan Bombonière

Candy-coated almonds are a popular and affordable favor. Their symbolism as the union of the sweet and the bitter has helped them endure through generations. But just because millions of people have given them as favors is no reason to avoid them—of course that's no reason to use them, either. If you like the underlying symbolism, by all means make them a small gift for your guests. If you like the idea of sweets for your guests, but you aren't keen on the typical (and tooth-breaking) goodie, use the best-wrapped chocolates you can find instead. The real key is to make your version just a little bit different than everyone else's. The standard is to grab a square of tulle, plop some Jordan almonds inside, gather it up, and tie with a ribbon or (really not our style) a rubber band. Yes, it's easy and, yes, it's what everyone does.

Our version may be a little more complicated, but on the difficulty scale, it still ranks as "able to do when you're brain-dead tired." We used two tones of tulle and small faux flowers to enhance the traditional.

1. Place the cake round over a piece of pink tulle and cut around the shape with scissors. Repeat the process with the green tulle.

2. Place a sheet of the round pink tulle on flat surface, then place the round green tulle on top of it. Place about eleven of the almonds in the center of the tulle.

3. Gather tulle tightly around the almonds, and tie off with a 12" (30.5 cm) length of ribbon. Tie ribbon in a bow then place a single flower in the center of the bow, wrapping wire around package, under the secured ribbon.

4. To finish off the free ends of the ribbon with style, pinch the ends in half length-wise (so the ribbon is narrower). Snip the ribbon with scissors held at a 45°angle. The finished end will look like a pennant tail. Repeat on other free end. Trim top of netting to neaten and finish edges.

TIP *Speaking of symbolism, wrap the candies (almond or others) in odd numbers. Because an odd number cannot be divided evenly in half, it is thought to symbolize the inseparability of the couple.*

MATERIALS

Pink and green tulle or netting

12" (30.5 cm) cardboard cake round

1/2" (1.3 cm) wide green silk ribbon

Packet of paper flowers with wire stem

Jordan almonds, pralined hazelnuts, or other yummies

Scissors

Flower Power Jewelry

BEADED RING, NECKLACE, AND BRACELET

**MATERIALS
FOR RING**

**One small
package
seed beads**

**Six 4 mm
crystal beads**

**Six 6 mm
crystal beads**

**One package
"no stretch" nylon
bead string, size # 4 in
coordinating color**

**One package of
clear stretchable
bead cord**

**Five bendable
bead needles
(small enough to
fit through a
seed bead)**

Needle-nose pliers

A tiny boutique in Barcelona sells a ring and bracelet similar to these. Never able to leave well enough alone, we came up with an adaptation that we like a little better—and a necklace to match.

The outstanding element of this jewelry is the stylized flower pattern that is not too delicate. Using crystal and glass beads instead of plastic keeps the colors clear and bright and adds a needed weight to the pieces. We used vibrant colors for our pieces that would be lively assets to your bridesmaids' outfits. These pieces also make a stunning gift for your mother or your future mother-in-law. For a lighter look, use clear and teal crystals together.

DIRECTIONS FOR RING

1. Thread 3 yards (2.7 m) of a single strand of bead string through the needle. Do not tie a knot at the end.

2. String six seed beads onto the thread, leaving about 2" (5.1 cm) of thread on the end *(see fig. 1)*.

3. Form a circle of beads by pushing the needle and thread back through the first bead *(see fig. 1)*.

4. String up one 4 mm crystal bead, followed by one 6 mm crystal bead, followed by another 4 mm crystal bead. These beads are labeled A, B, and C in *fig. 2* .

5. Pull thread taut and wrap around the thread that runs in between seed beads five and six *(see fig. 3)*. Pull needle back through crystal bead C. Pull taut. Crystal beads A and C will look perpendicular to seed bead circle. Bead B will be parallel to seed bead circle.

TIP *Bring a swatch of the bridesmaids' dress fabric to the bead store so you can coordinate the colors. You could also make these in shades of cream, white or whatever color you choose for your own wedding dress.*

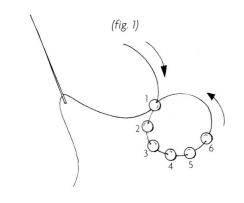

(fig. 1)

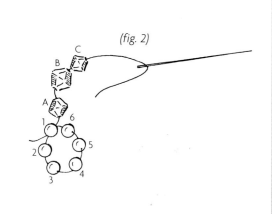

(fig. 2)

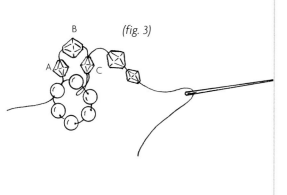

(fig. 3)

6. Add on another 6 mm crystal bead, followed by another 4 mm crystal bead and repeat the same process, this time wrapping needle and thread around existing thread in between seed beads five and four, then going back through the 4 mm crystal until you have formed the second petal.

7. Repeat this process until you have all six of the 6 mm crystals and all six of the 4 mm beads in place and have created the flower. Finish off flower by inserting the needle through the top of the first 4 mm bead.

8. Solidify the flower by running the needle and thread in a circle in through the holes of the 6 mm beads. Work your needle through the piece until it meets with the loose 2" (5.1 cm) end that you left hanging when you started your seed bead circle. Tie a square knot with your two end pieces. Weave the existing ends through the beads and then trim. The flower face should form a slight dome once the thread is pulled taut and tied off.

9. For the band, cut approximately 1 yard (.9 m) of the stretchable cord and single thread through eye of a bendable needle. Attach to flower by wrapping around thread in between two of the 6 mm beads on the outside edge of the flower. Leave 2" (5.1 cm) on the end for tying off later.

10. String on twenty-seven seed beads and insert needle on opposite side of flower (three 6 mm beads away), looping stretch thread around existing thread on flower in between two beads. Pull thread taut.

11. Place another twenty-seven seed beads onto the needle and bring the needle back through the original point where you began the band. Make a square knot with two ends of cord. Pull knot tight with needle-nose pliers and cut ends close. You could put a little dab of Super Glue onto the knot to secure it.

DIRECTIONS FOR NECKLACE

1. Make the center flower of the ring by following steps one through eight of the ring directions.

2. Add jump ring onto the piece by placing around the thread in between two beads. Close up with needle-nose pliers.

3. To make the ribbon necklace, cut a 20" (50.8 cm) length of ribbon, making sure to square up the edges of the ribbon as best as possible with the scissors. Thread 12" (30.5 cm) of

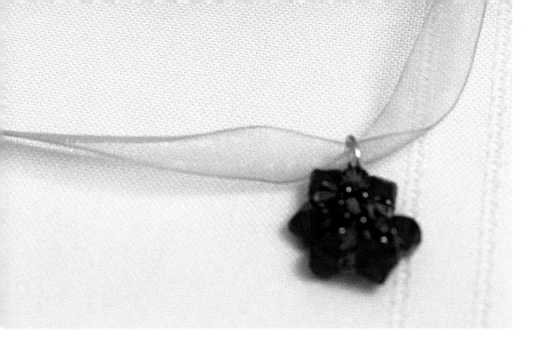

**MATERIALS
FOR NECKLACE**

**24" (61 cm) of ³⁄₈" (1 cm)
colored silk organza or
organdy ribbon**

**Two medium
gold jump rings**

One gold jewelry clasp

Two gold bead tips

**One small package
seed beads**

Two bead tips

Six 4 mm crystal beads

Six 6 mm crystal beads

**One package "no stretch"
nylon bead string, size # 4
in coordinating color**

**Five bendable bead
needles (small enough
to fit through seed bead)**

**One regular
sewing needle**

Needle-nose pliers

bead string onto the regular sewing needle. Knot the end of the bead string and run it through one end of the ribbon.

4. Run the ribbon and needle and thread through the hole in the bead tip, making sure to pull the entire end of the ribbon through the hole *(see fig. 4)*. Tie a few more knots at the end of the bead string to prevent the ribbon from slipping out of the bead tip. Cut the string and close up the bead tip with the needle-nose pliers.

5. Thread the free end of the ribbon through the flower pendant jump ring.

6. Repeat step four on the other end of the ribbon. Add a jump ring on one end of bead tip and clasp on other end. Close up jump ring with needle-nose pliers and your necklace is complete.

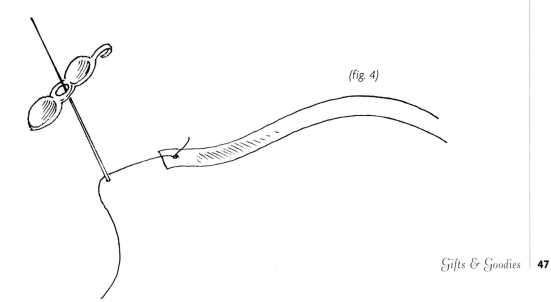

(fig. 4)

MATERIALS FOR BRACELET

Small seed beads

Small beads, just larger than seed beads, but large enough to accommodate three strands of wire through the hole

6 mm crystal beads

Fine beading wire

Two jump rings

Bracelet clasp

Needle-nose pliers

Scissors

DIRECTIONS FOR BRACELET

1. Cut three yard-long (meter-long) strands of beading wire. Twist the strands together on one end. Thread two medium beads onto the wires.

2. On the right and left strands, thread on nine seed beads. On the middle strand, thread one medium bead, one crystal, and another medium bead *(see fig. 5)*.

VARIATION *This design also works great as a choker. Wrap a dressmaker's measuring tape around your neck to determine the length. Add a small length of chain to the end of the necklace to vary the size.*

3. Twist the three strands together twice, keeping the beads close together. Thread two medium beads onto the twisted strands. Separate the wires, and thread on beads as in step two *(see fig. 6)*.

4. Repeat the process until the bracelet measures a little longer than the size of the wearer's wrist. Both ends should be twisted, so the beading stays tight. Wrap each end around a jump ring and twist the wire back on itself to secure it. You can add a chain to one end for variable lengths.

5. Trim the excess. Attach the clasp pieces to the jump rings with needle-nose pliers.

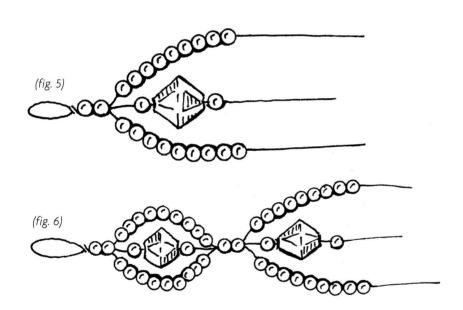

(fig. 5)

(fig. 6)

Mooning Over Memories

PAPER AND MOONSTONE FRAME

All too often the words "elegant" and "expensive" are used interchangeably. We know that you are horrified, too. Although some elegant items are amazingly expensive, the two are not inextricably linked—a mistake that is made over and over again, especially when weddings are concerned. We have faith that you can tell the difference. If you wonder if a designer hand-cut glass frame might go over better than this one, simply because it's costly, don't be too sure. (If you find yourself actually asking that question, it's time for an intervention.) People who like cut glass will prefer it, but the simplicity of this frame makes it striking.

Picture frames are a popular gift because they invite recipients to remember friends and family. However, they can be very expensive, especially when you are looking for something special. Instead of spending a bundle on frames that anyone can find, buy basic and transform it into a work of art itself. There won't be any others like it and the end result will have a prominent place in your friends' homes.

You can give the frame complete with a picture of the future bride and groom. Or, insert your favorite photo of you and the recipient.

VARIATION *You don't have to stick to small frames. Huge frames with small openings look stunning when combined with a subtly decorated paper. This technique works with any size frame as long as your paper is big enough. If you are having trouble finding paper big enough, consider wallpaper or wrapping paper.*

MATERIALS

One picture frame with flat surface and a 5" × 7" (12.7 cm × 17.8 cm) opening

One sheet 20" × 30" (50.8 cm × 76.2 cm) decorative paper

Roundstone sequins

Bone folder

Spray adhesive

Craft knife

Metal ruler

Sharp pencil

Craft glue

Cotton swab

1. Place sheet of decorative paper face down on cutting surface.

2. Remove glass and backing from picture frame and place frame face down, centering it on paper.

3. Draw a pencil line around outer edge of frame. Remove frame and place to the side.

4. Measure a rectangle that is one inch larger than the existing rectangle on all sides. Mark it with a pencil.

5. Cut out larger rectangle with a craft knife.

6. Place decorative paper face down on work surface and spray it with spray mount.

7. Center frame face down over paper.

8. Turn face up and burnish out any bubbles with your bone folder.

9. Turn face down and trim corners with craft knife as follows: Left and right edges can be cut square at 90° angles. Top and bottom edges should be cut at a 45° angle *(see fig. 1)*.

10. Fold in left and right edges of decorative paper to back of frame, scoring edges with bone folder and burnishing as you adhere them to the back of the frame.

11. Fold in top edges to back of frame in similar fashion.

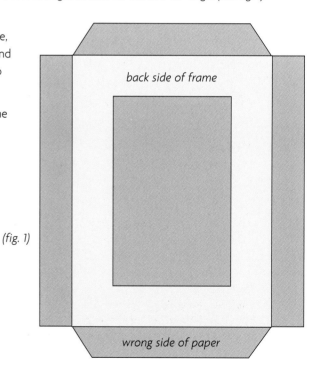

(fig. 1)

back side of frame

wrong side of paper

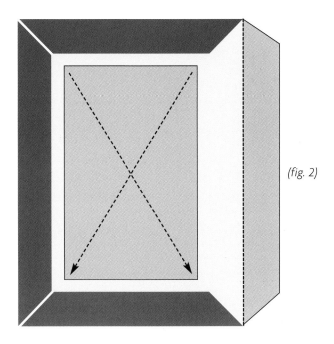

(fig. 2)

12. Cut an opening for the photo with a craft knife. Start in the upper left-hand corner and cut to the lower right-hand corner. Then cut from the upper right-hand corner to the lower left *(see fig. 2)*.

13. Fold the paper flaps to the back side of the frame, scoring and burnishing the paper with your bone folder. Trim excess paper with craft knife.

14. Turn frame face up on the work surface. Finish off the inside corners by adding seven round-stones to each corner. Apply with cotton swab and a small dab of craft glue. Start with one at each corner and work your way out left and right until all seven have been placed. Use your craft knife to coax the moonstones into place.

15. Trim your favorite picture to fit. Clean the glass and put it back in the frame. Place photo and backing on frame.

TIP *You can use a paper that picks up some color, pattern, or feeling of the wedding itself. A lovely paper from your invitation will forever be echoed in the frame. Or, perhaps the dark olive tones of the restaurant's cashmere walls and teal beaded lights will resonate in a deep green paper and teal stones.*

Guest Survival Kit

MATERIALS

Mini lunch boxes, one for each room

Scissors

Adhesive-backed printer paper

Template from page 124

Color photocopier or scanner and color printer

CONTENTS FOR THE KIT

Maps, directions, sewing kit, itinerary, list of guests, travel toothbrush, trail mix, brownies, and so on

When friends travel from out of town for a wedding, they immediately feel welcomed and excited about the festivities when they find these special packages waiting in their hotel rooms. A survival kit should include the basics for the weekend: maps (with locations highlighted), directions, and a schedule of events. Include some other useful items like a sewing kit, bottle opener, or travel toothbrush.

Add munchies for the late-night snack attacks as well as a special something from your favorite nearby bakery. Place the baked goods in a glassine or waxed paper envelope and seal with directions to the bakery so your friends can get their early morning java fix without feeling helpless. Complete the kit with a personal note and any amenities your friends might love, such as a great bath product, a sidecar bottle of wine, an eye mask, or a stuffed animal for the kids.

Talk to the hotel manager about the guest packages when you are arranging the reservations. On the morning of the arrival date, drop the packages at the hotel with name tags attached.

1. Print Guest Survival Kit logos on adhesive paper. Make color photocopies of the logo on page 124, or scan it into your computer and print copies in color. You can fit about eight on a page.

2. Cut out the Guest Survival Kit logos from the sticker paper.

3. Place the stickers on the lunch boxes.

4. Fill with contents, placing the munchies and note on top of the stack.

5. Tie a name tag on the handle and deliver the packages to the hotel.

VARIATION *If you can't find plain, inexpensive lunch boxes, check card stores for small, handled gift bags. Tie the handles together with the name tag and some curled ribbon.*

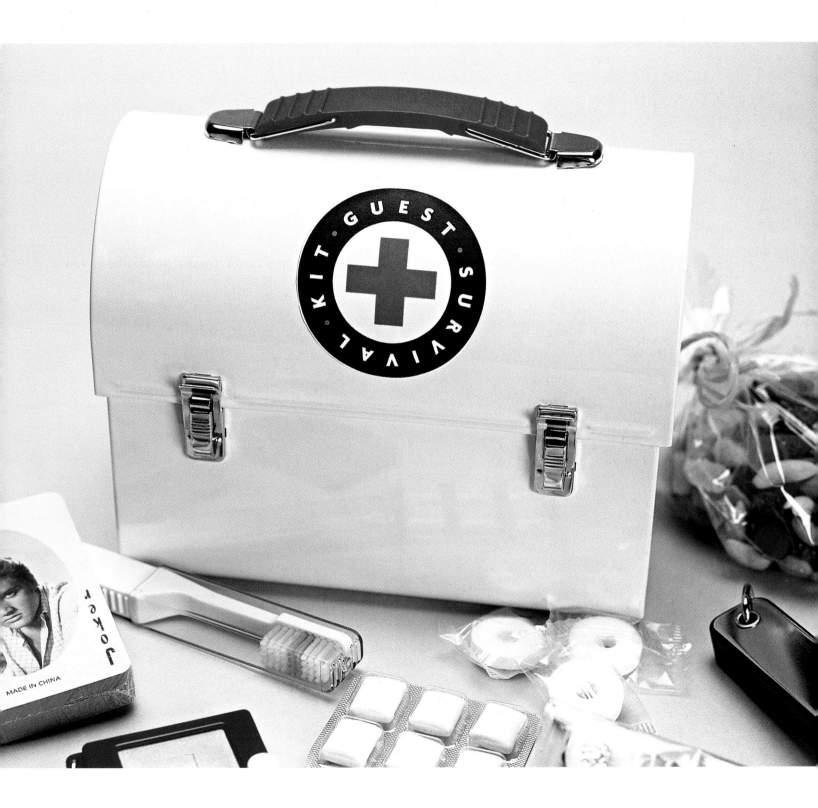

brian + pam

songs from our wedding 9.5.03

The Beat Goes On

MUSIC CD

Music is part of the scene. Whether it's Ella and Louis crooning during dinner or the best funk band in Pittsburgh blaring their horns across the crowded dance floor, music locks an event in memory. Send guests on their way with a melodic favor that will find a permanent home in their CD players.

Use your computer savvy to make a compilation of music, either from your wedding day or that you two have enjoyed together. Make a label and case insert and you have a swell-looking CD.

MATERIALS

Personal computer

Color printer

CD burner

CD-R blank CDs (the kind you can burn in a computer or CD burner)

Plain CD jewel cases

Gloss white or silver foil adhesive CD labels that work with your model color printer

Photo-quality paper, 8 1/2" × 11" (21.6 cm × 27.9 cm)

Craft knife or paper trimmer

Ruler

Bone folder

TO MAKE THE CD

1. Using a CD burner and the program installed on your computer, create a compilation and burn the CD. Allow yourself enough time to figure out the process, if you haven't done it before.

2. Listen to a few of the CDs to make sure there isn't a problem with the data transfer. Pop each CD into a jewel case and start on the inserts.

TO MAKE THE CD CASE INSERT AND LABEL

1. Using your favorite graphics program, create a horizontal document that is 9 $^7/_{16}$" x 4 $^{11}/_{16}$" (23.9 cm x 11.9 cm). The left half of the document will be the inside cover of your CD case. Choosing your favorite typeface and colors, write a list of the songs. You can also include a message from both of you to your guests—but you should keep it simple.

2. The right half of the document will be the cover of the CD case. Choose a favorite image, and give your CD a title. Print the inserts on photo-quality paper. Cut out the insert using a craft knife and a ruler or a paper trimmer. Fold the inserts in half and score with a bone folder. Slide the inserts into the inside covers of the CD jewel cases.

3. Arrange the cover photo and text to print on a CD label. Print a draft to line up everything. Print finished labels and stick on to burned CD.

TIP *Listen carefully to the words and sentiments of the songs you choose. There are plenty of great songs that are not emblematic of your wedding wishes. Even if you love "Boulevard of Broken Dreams," save it for a different CD. You don't have to be tame, but give some thought to the lyrics.*

Cuppa Quiet

PAINT-YOUR-OWN-POTTERY TEA KIT

MATERIALS

An idea for a design, simpler is better

A selection of teas and tea accessories to fit inside the cup

Interesting paper

Decorative-edge scissors

Small hole punch

String

Sometimes a quiet evening with a hot cup of tea is just the relaxation we need when life gets busy. That goes for both you and your friends. Give your shower guests or bridal party a lead on an evening curled up with a hot cuppa and a book. Start at a paint-your-own-pottery store and pick out the biggest latte cups they have. Take along a Walkman and enjoy the time to yourself (with your busy life, you know how rare that is already). You can personalize them for each guest. After a few days, your creations will be ready to pick up. Fill them with your favorite selection of teas. Add some crystal sugar and a book to round out the gift.

1. Sketch out your design on the cup and saucer with a regular No. 2 pencil. The marks from this pencil will burn off in the firing process. If you want a mark that will show after firing, ask for an underglaze pencil.

2. Paint your design with the underglaze paints. You will need three to four coats for a vibrant finished project, or one to two coats for a watercolor look. Many stores have squeeze bottles of paints for writing, so you can add names, dates, and messages to your design. Leave the cups and saucers to be fired. They should be ready in a few days.

3. Fill the cup with teas and accessories. Choose either favorites or something straightforward and simple, like an English Breakfast or Earl Grey. For a special treat, try the amazing teas from Mariage Frères in Paris. You can order them by mail (see Resources, page 126).

4. Cut a 1" x 1" (2.5 cm x 2.5 cm) square of paper with the decorative-edge scissors. Punch a small hole in the tag and thread a string through it, anchored with a knot. Write a message on the tag and tape the end of the string inside the cup, lopping the tag over the rim.

SHORTCUT *Don't fret if you don't have a lot of time. You can buy nicely decorated latte cups, too. Just apply your creativity to the label and contents.*

Knickers with a Twist

PERSONALIZED PANTIES FOR YOUR PALS

MATERIALS FOR SCOUT PATCH

"Scout green" underwear

Girl Scout or Boy Scout patches

Matching thread

Needle

Scissors

Straight pins

Beautiful articles with age-old refinement make terrific gifts. But for your closest friends, familiarity and humor count the most. Forget the garish lingerie that often circulates at these occasions and opt for a wittier approach. These undies may be a little daring, but they are going to your nearest gal pals…who will most certainly get a laugh. All you need is a little inventiveness and a willingness to exploit some pure and wholesome materials.

Personalize your pit crew's (a.k.a bridesmaids') undies with a homemade gas station attendant's patch. Simply handwrite each of the bridesmaid's names on the patches and do a basic backstitch in embroidery thread. Or sew on a bowling patch and your girlfriends will have a spare to go with their Campers and bowling shirts. You can even give out some merit badges to the gals that deserve them the most (your scout troop was always prepared, you know). If patches are not readily available in your area, log onto to eBay.com, look under patches, and play to win. This project works great with boxers, too!

DIRECTIONS FOR SCOUT PATCH

1. Align patches on front of underwear and pin in place.
2. Sew patches on underwear.
3. Trim threads with scissors.

TIP *Complete the gift by packaging the undies in containers that go with the theme. The scout panties can be wrapped in a bandana, the gas station attendant's in a funnel, and the bowling undies in a bowling bag.*

**MATERIALS FOR
BOWLING PATCH**

Black underwear

Bowling patch

Matching thread

Needle

Scissors

Straight pins

**Red embroidery
thread**

Embroidery needle

Tracing paper

Pencil

DIRECTIONS FOR BOWLING PATCH

1. Align patch on front of underwear and pin in place.

2. Sew patch on underwear.

3. Trim threads with scissors.

4. Handwrite attendant's name in cursive on tracing paper in pencil. Center paper under bowling ball patch and pin into place.

5. Thread about 3 yards (2.7 m) of single-thread embroidery floss through the embroidery needle. Pull the needle up through the beginning of your letter form, leaving about 1" (2.5 cm) of loose thread. Do not tie off.

6. Embroider the name through the layer of tracing paper. Do a simple backstitch until you've completed embroidering the name. Do not tie off the end. Weave the thread back through your piece to secure ends. Trim both ends of loose thread.

7. Pull off tracing paper layer.

DIRECTIONS FOR GAS STATION ATTENDANT PATCH

1. Copy oval template from page 124. Center over twill iron-on patch. Pin in place and cut out shape. Place a piece of tracing paper over the patch and trace the outline of the shape. Handwrite attendant's name in cursive on the tracing paper oval in pencil, centering the name in the oval as best you can.

2. Pin the oval tracing paper to the oval twill patch.

3. Thread about 3 yards (2.7 m) of single-thread embroidery floss through the embroidery needle. Pull needle up through the beginning of your letter form, leaving about 1" (2.5 cm) of loose thread. Do not tie off.

4. Embroider the name through the layer of tracing paper. Do a simple backstitch until you've completed embroidering the name. Do not tie off the end. Weave the thread back through your piece to secure ends. Trim both ends of loose thread.

5. Pull off tracing paper layer.

6. Preheat iron for 8 minutes. Do not add water. Iron underwear flat.

7. Position patch on underwear front and iron onto panty. Make sure you do not iron the elastic waistband because it will melt.

8. Measure out a 12" (30.5 cm) length of the soutache braid and place along outer edge of patch.

9. Take braid off patch and place to the side. Run a thin line of fabric glue along outer edge of patch. Starting at center bottom, place braid around edge and glue into place. The ends may fray a little, so put an extra dab of glue at the ends to stop this from happening. Overlap the ends a tiny bit and trim to fit. Let glue set about 20 minutes.

10. Topstitch soutache braid in place either by hand or with a machine.

VARIATION *Customize the patches to your friends' personalities and tastes. Most sewing and army and navy stores offer a wide array of patches with which you can coordinate the panty colors.*

MATERIALS FOR GAS STATION ATTENDANT PATCH

Dark blue cotton underwear

White or off-white twill iron-on patches

Oval template from page 124

Tracing paper

Pencil

3/32" (2.4 mm) red no-iron soutache braid

Red embroidery thread

Embroidery needle

Fabric glue

Red sewing thread

Sewing needle

Scissors

Straight pins

MATERIALS

4" × 6" × 3/4"
(10.2 cm × 15.2 cm × 1.9 cm) cardboard gift box

4" × 6"
(10.2 cm × 15.2 cm) sheet of 1/16" thick (1.6 cm) Plexiglas

Spray adhesive

Craft knife

Red book cloth

Drafting triangle

Metal ruler

Pencil

Template from page 124

Color photocopier or scanner and printer

8 1/2" × 11"
(21.6 cm × 27.9 cm) glossy photo paper

Awl

Three 4 mm ball bearings

Black fine-tip permanent marker

Bone folder

Small container of adhesive solvent, such as Bestine

Cotton swab

Maybe, Baby!
RETRO BALL BEARING TOY

Most guests will recognize the familiar sound of this toy, the soft sound of steel balls rolling on paperboard in search of the high score. Combine that with a groan of exasperation followed by a whoop of success, and you complete the memory. The retro design of this favor is perfect for this age-old occasion and gives people a little something to fidget with during conversations or a break in dancing. Instead of a maze or rockets heading to space, this toy features a comic book–style matrimony moment. If, however, you prefer rockets heading to space….

1. Color photocopy the illustration from page 124 onto high-quality paper stock. Or scan it and print it on your color printer, on glossy photo paper. Trim edges with craft knife and ruler.

2. Pierce a hole in each of the "Yes," "No," and "Maybe" circles with an awl. Color in any rough edges with the black marker.

3. Spray mount back of the illustration and paste it into the box. Drop in the three ball bearings.

4. Measure, then cut out a piece of 6" x 8" (15.2 cm x 20.3 cm) book cloth, using pencil, triangle, ruler, and craft knife.

5. Lay fabric wrong side up. Place box in dead center of material and trace the outside of the box onto the fabric with a pencil.

VARIATION *You may want to make up your own graphic, use a photo, or find a postcard. Use your imagination to customize the game to your own taste.*

(fig. 1)

fold flap in

(fig. 2)

6. Spray mount the wrong side of the material. Return box to dead center and burnish it in place with the bone folder. Then turn right-side up and place the Plexiglas on top of box.

7. Cut fabric corners on the short sides at 90° angles and long sides at 45° angles *(see fig. 1)*.

8. Fold and burnish material onto long sides of box with your bone folder. Fold and burnish material onto short sides of box. *(see fig. 2)*.

9. Continue folding and burnishing onto the Plexiglas top of the box. Trim corners at a 45° angle.

10. Trim border on top to about 1/8" (3 mm) with craft knife and metal ruler.

11. Clean off excess adhesive with Bestine and a cotton swab.

Adapting Style

No doubt about it. You've got style. The great thing about your style is that it gives you a trademark to stamp on everything. A wedding is the best time to let your style be your guide. Of course, we're in favor of letting your style guide you all the time, from the pen you use to the eyeglasses you wear. At a wedding, you host a gathering for a special reason, and every bit of it should let guests know that it is your wedding. That is, yours and your fiancé's. What good is a wedding—a union—if it only reflects the style of one of you? Not very stylish at all, we think.

CHANGING PROJECTS TO FIT

Adapting a project to fit your style isn't very hard at all. At first it may feel difficult, because projects list materials and colors...and (you might think) pretty much dictate a style. But the materials lists are meant to be changed. The projects are inspiration waiting for your direction, to adapt them to fit your needs and your style. Change the papers used to those that you think are beautiful, or those that go with the season. Change any element to make it more your own.

If a project is too floral for you, you don't have to eliminate the project from your repertoire—change the flowers into dots, clouds, or whatever is up your alley. If you already have an invitation ordered from your favorite stationers, look at invitation projects in a different light, instead of skipping over them. The same concept can be adapted to make a mini photo album cover, a menu, a welcome card to place in a hotel room, or a program. Let your brain play with projects and develop ways to to fit your needs. These projects can be taken apart and re-created as your own.

BALANCING STYLES

It takes a little work to identify your particular style—especially if it is eclectic. You might like woodsy items and lace, as well as pop items that add humor and modern style. The key to making it all work is to find a balance.

If you like flowers, you *could* make everything floral—but that would be overkill. The flowers might invade everything and lose their significance or beauty. Balance the textures and bright colors of flowers with smooth lines and sleek colors. A smooth silver iZone guest book (see page 114) used in a flower-heavy wedding will stand out as an elegant and fun item. At the same time it will give the flowers a greater effect on the setting.

Likewise, if you opt for all pop and kitsch, your wedding and reception could feel cold and even sarcastic. Warm it up by adding a touch of the opposite style: Add a small cut flower to each place assignment chair (see page 118) or use a woodsy paper on the card box (see page 106). Subtly blending in other textures balances the effect. Lines are softened, heavy textures are tempered with elegance and sleek additions. Guests will feel at ease because your style is balanced. ❋

3 Ceremony Details

A wedding ceremony is a personal moment you share with those closest to you—unless you've invited 1,000 people. More importantly, it's a time you share with the one person closest to you, and the ceremony details should fit both of you. Not surprisingly, many ceremony details are dictated by the officiating body. Depending on where you've chosen to get married, and by whom, you may have to adhere to certain guidelines. Some places may insist that you leave a pause for anyone to object (despite *your* objection to the idea), others may not let your best-friend-opera-star sing a note. But you can always find those that will even let you have a juggler if you so desire (why not?). We feel pretty confident that you'll check out the entire ceremony to make sure you get what you want. After all, there's no sense in paying attention to the details if you don't look at the overall experience as well. The result of your efforts will be a meaningful ceremony that highlights the essence of your personalities and your shared history.

But once the mechanics of the ceremony are addressed, how can you personalize the look? We assembled some details that will add your own style to the standard elements. When you pick out your dress, the flowers, and the menswear, the easiest element for a unique twist is you. For that reason, we've designed some jewelry, headwear, and shoes for you to adapt to your colors or style. We've also included a pillow the ring bearer will be glad to hold.

MATERIALS

¹/₄ (22.9 cm) yard
cotton poplin

Scissors

1 yard (.9 m) of 4 ¹/₂"
(11.4 cm) wide light
blue organdy
or organza ribbon

1 yard (.9 m) of 4 ¹/₂"
(11.4 cm) wide
white organdy or
organza ribbon

1 yard (.9 m) of ¹/₄"
(6.4 mm) wide
light blue organdy
or organza ribbon

Straight pins

Small bag cotton
pillow stuffing

Silver seed beads

Tin letters
"L, O, V, E"

White
sewing thread

Needle

Sewing machine

Drafting triangle

Ruler

Sewing pencil
or marker

Cushion of Love

RING BEARER'S PILLOW

What can one say about the function of a ring bearer's pillow? Usually not much beyond its status as the highly guarded accessory of one young wedding participant. What makes this pillow so special? The punched tin letters juxtaposed against the fragile-looking organza and sparkly seed beads adds an unexpected industrial edge to a delicate, soft object. You can read into the combination of opposites all you like, we won't object. But the overall effect is that the word "LOVE" pops out very well because it is a sharper, cooler material than the background.

1. Measure and cut an 8" (20.3 cm) square of cotton poplin.

2. Measure and cut two 8" (20.3 cm) strips of the 4¹/₂" (11.4 cm) wide white ribbon and two 8" (20.3 cm) strips of the blue ribbon.

3. Basket weave the four strips together. Lay one white ribbon vertically on the work surface. Lay one blue ribbon horizontally over the white ribbon. Lay the second white ribbon vertically to the left of the first white ribbon. Lay the second blue ribbon parallel to the other blue ribbon. Flip up the end of the first white ribbon and lay it over the second blue ribbon. The ribbons will form what looks like four quadrants. Pin these together with straight pins.

VARIATION *For a more personalized approach, substitute the word "LOVE" with the bride and groom's first and last initials.*

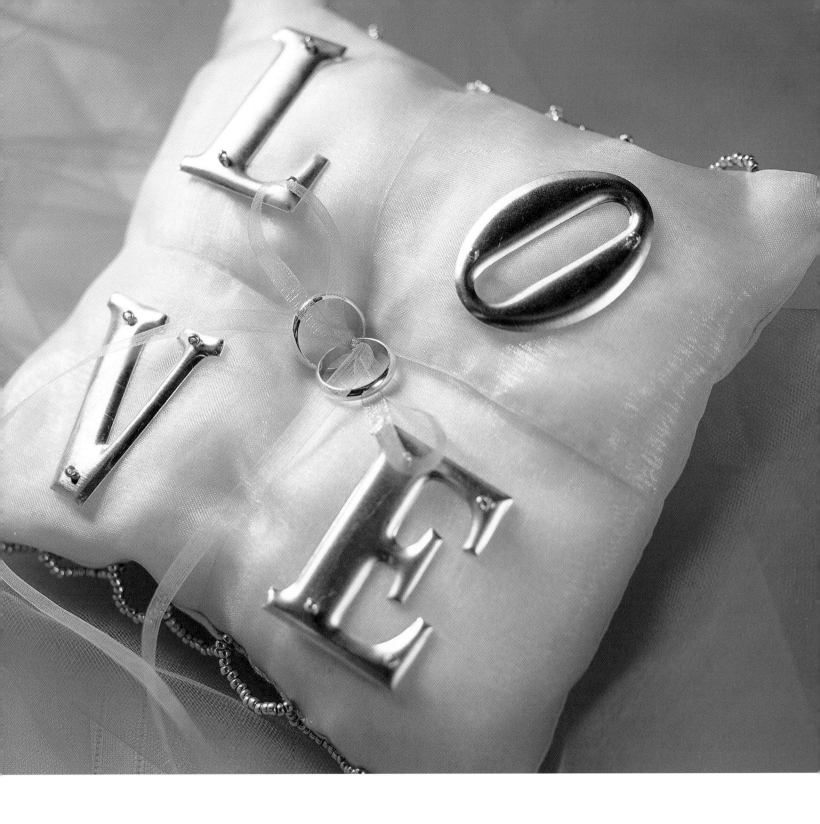

4. Topstitch the ribbons onto a cotton square, leaving about $^3/_8$" (1 cm) all around.

5. Center, then hand sew the letters "L, O, V, and E" to each of the quadrants of the ribbon so it matches the photograph: Start sewing through the bottom of the ribbon, then through the letter hole. Thread a seed bead onto the needle. Go back through the letter hole again and knot and cut the ends. Continue this process until all the letters have been sewn onto the ribbon.

6. Place letter side of fabric face down over other cotton square. Pin two sides together.

7. Sew a $^1/_2$" (1.3 cm) seam all around, leaving a 3 $^1/_2$" (8.9 cm) seam opening along the bottom edge to turn the piece right-side out. Trim the corners of the newly sewn seam to reduce fabric bulk. Turn the pillow right-side out.

8. Stuff the pillow and blind stitch the seam opening.

TIP *You can use either gold or silver seed beads to accent the piece. Gold seed beads would coordinate best with gold rings, silver seed beads with platinum rings.*

9. Make tick marks every ³⁄₄" (1.9 cm) on top and bottom edges of pillow. Thread 2 yards (1.8 m) of a double strand of thread on the needle. Insert needle into pillow's lower left corner and knot the loose end. String up fifteen seed beads, then sew back into pillow at first tick mark *(see fig. 1)* Continue doing this, creating a scalloped pattern until you've reached the lower right corner of the pillow. Do the same on top of the pillow. Knot and trim ends.

10. Sew the center point of the ¼" (6.4 mm) wide blue ribbon into the center of the pillow. Pass the needle and thread through all of the layers of batting and fabric. Leave the loose end on top of the pillow without tying the loose end. On the back side of the pillow, thread a seed bead through the needle. Then pass the needle back through all the layers of the pillow. Sew through the center point of the ¼" (6.4 mm) ribbon, through a seed bead and back through the ribbon. Tie both thread loose ends together on the underside of the ribbon. Make sure the ribbon feels very secure, as it will be holding your rings.

11. Thread your rings onto the ribbon and tie it in a bow.

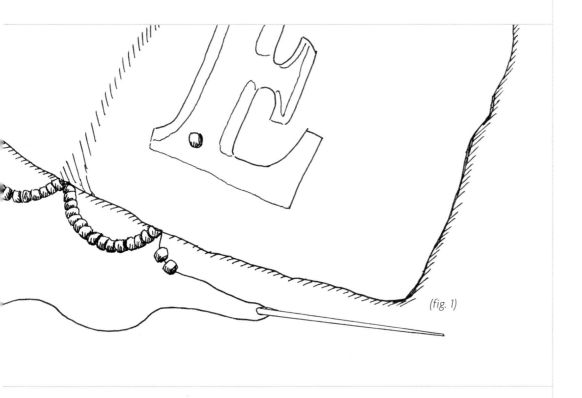

(fig. 1)

Practical Princess-Wear

SUBTLE TIARA

Everyone should have a tiara to wear to state dinners, shopping, and baseball games. For your wedding, it should be a very nice one. Put Harry Winston's on hold (not that any of us want to, mind you), and craft your own that will look sensible and delicate without the need for an armed escort. The materials and method are incredibly simple, but the finished product won't show that at all.

1. Use the measuring tape to find the center point of your headband.

2. Pull out about 3 yards (2.7 m) of wire. Wrap the center of the wire once around the center of the band (see fig. 1).

3. String on five seed beads (this may vary according to the width of your band). Wrap around width of headband and to the right of the center point. Pull tightly. The five seed beads should cover the width of the headband. You may need more or fewer beads for each wraparound.

4. Wrap wire around headband tightly again, this time without adding on the five seed beads. This will secure the beads.

5. Continue steps three and four (see figs. 2-3), wrapping wire and adding beads until you have fifty rows of seed beads. Make sure bead rows rest snuggly against each other, without wire showing through. Secure wire on end by wrapping it back through the piece in between the bead rows three or four times. Cut end and tuck in between bead rows using your fingernail to wedge it into place.

6. Starting back at the center point, repeat steps two through five, this time working the other side of the center point.

TIP *If you want to wear a veil with the tiara, sew the veil onto both ends of your beadwork.*

MATERIALS

One spool heavy-guage craft wire

One white or cream cloth-covered headband with boning inside

One container white seed beads

Twenty 4 mm silver and clear crystals

Ten 6 mm clear crystals

Sewing measuring tape

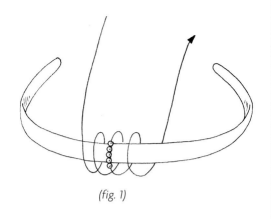

(fig. 1)

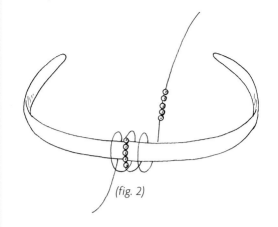

(fig. 2)

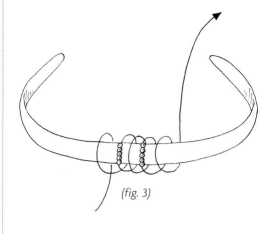

(fig. 3)

7. You are now ready to top the tiara. Starting on the left-hand side of the piece, wrap the wire around the headband once or twice, securing it between bead rows.

8. Add on six white seed beads followed by one 4 mm crystal, followed by one 6 mm crystal, followed by another 4 mm crystal, followed by six more seed beads *(see fig. 4)*.

9. Count in ten rows from the end of the headband and wrap the wire around the headband between rows ten and eleven *(see fig. 5)*.

10. Add on six more white seed beads followed by one 4 mm crystal, followed by one 6 mm crystal, followed by another 4 mm crystal, followed by six more seed beads. Wrap wire around between rows twenty and twenty-one.

11. Repeat this process, wrapping around every tenth row until you and make it to row one hundred.

12. Secure wire on end by wrapping it back through the piece between the bead rows three or four times. Cut end and tuck in between bead rows using your fingernail to wedge it into place.

VARIATION *Use colored beads to match the color of your dress. Ivory-colored seed beads with clear peach crystals are a great combination for an ivory-colored dress.*

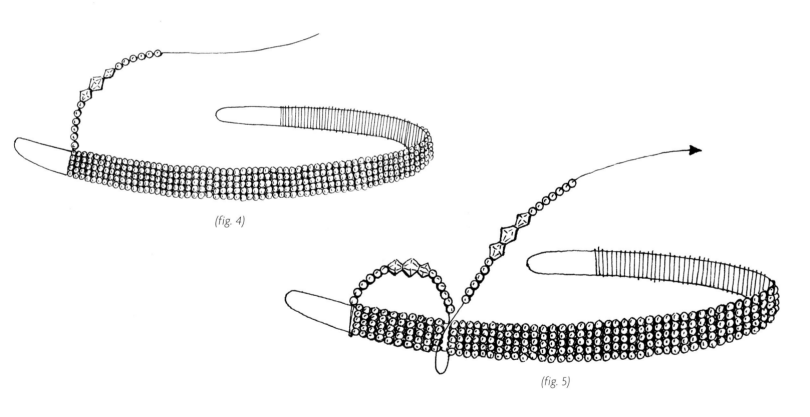

(fig. 4)

(fig. 5)

Twinkle Toes

SHOE DECORATIONS

**MATERIALS FOR
BEADED SHOE**

**One pair of
wedding sandals**

**Four cream or
white silk leaves with
wire stems**

**28-gauge
beading wire**

**Ten pink
freshwater pearls**

**Small container
of silver seed beads**

**Small container of
white seed beads**

**Small container of
clear seed beads**

Scissors

Flowers are lively accents—especially when peeking out from beneath the hem of a long dress. Even though your feet may feel like wilting after the long evening you have planned, real flowers would fall flat much sooner than that. Silk flowers will survive the scuffle of a march down the aisle and multiple turns on the dance floor.

DIRECTIONS FOR BEADED SHOE

1. Pull out about 2 yards (1.8 m) of beading wire and cut.

2. String five freshwater pearls and form a circle, leaving 2" (5.1 cm) of loose wire on the end.

3. Overlap short end of wire and pull the circle tight (see fig. 1).

4. Add five silver seed beads to the long end of wire (see fig. 2).

5. Wrap wire around other side of freshwater pearl, in between pearls one and two and pull wire tight.

6. Add five more silver beads and repeat the process, this time wrapping wire around between beads two and three (see fig. 3).

7. Add five more silver beads and repeat the process again, going in between beads three and four, and so on until you've completed the circle. Wrap wire around and tighten between beads one and five.

8. String an assortment of clear and white seed beads until you have strung up eleven beads onto the bead wire.

9. Wrap the wire around between beads one and two and pull wire tight. Repeat this process again and again until you have completed a full circle (see fig. 4).

TIP *Look for a shoe that has a somewhat narrow, simple band on the front. It will be easier to wrap the wire around and will show off the shoe decoration better.*

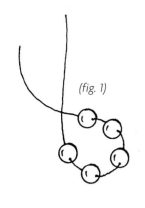

(fig. 1)

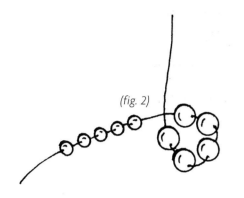

(fig. 2)

10. Weave long end of wire back through the piece to reinforce and stabilize the beaded flower.

11. Join wire ends together and tie off. Do not cut long end of wire.

12. Wire on one freshwater pearl to the center of the flower and weave through piece on underside to secure.

13. Cut silk leaves to desired size. Place horizontally on sandal front making a mirror image of the leaves on either side, leaves facing out, stems facing in. Wrap stems around midpoint of sandal front.

14. Add flower to center front of sandal and wrap around sandal with remaining wire from step eleven. When flower is secure, wrap a little remaining wire under the flower and trim wire end.

15. Repeat on second shoe and get ready to strut down that aisle.

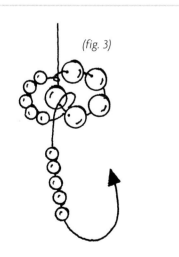

(fig. 3)

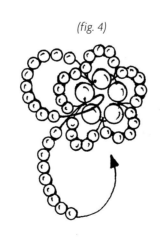

(fig. 4)

MATERIALS FOR SILK FLOWER FOOTWEAR

One pair of wedding sandals

Two white silk flowers, no larger than 3" (7.6 cm) when flattened

Two daisy party favor flowers

Two green silk leaves with wire stems

28-gauge beading wire

Scissors

DIRECTIONS FOR SILK FLOWER FOOTWEAR

1. Remove stems, pistils, and stamens from flowers, leaving just the petals.

2. Insert daisy into center of flower and wrap remaining daisy wire around front part of sandal.

3. Cut silk leaves down to desired size and twist stems under flower base.

4. Use additional beading wire to further reinforce flower and leaves onto shoe.

5. Repeat process on second shoe.

Dynamic Collier

METAL AND BEAD CHOKER

This stunning wire-and-bead choker necklace assures a one-of-a-kind ensemble. Of course, every bride wants to look unique. Although you'll look divine in a simple pearl necklace, some outfits cry out for a gutsier approach—and we're all for that.

We used silver wire for our necklace, but choose the metal color that matches your jewelry (gold if your rings are gold, silver if they are platinum), and have fun with the making. Try it on at your dress fitting to make sure the necklines go well together. If you can't get past the idea of doing without pearls, but you long for jewelry that is more exciting than a strand, brava! Just use freshwater pearl beads like we did here, available at finer bead supply stores.

1. Measure out and cut three strands of silver beading wire approximately 1 ½ yards (1.4 m) each.

2. Loop and twist about 3" (7.6 cm) of the wire on the end *(see fig. 1)*.

3. Add six silver seed beads onto the left wire. Add six silver seed beads onto the right wire. String one pearl onto the center wire.

4. Gather beads as tightly as you can, twisting the wire tightly four times to hold the beads in place *(see fig. 2)*.

5. Add a 4 mm crystal onto the right wire leaving about ¼" (6.4 mm) of slack on your wire *(see fig. 3)*.

6. Fold the wire back to last twisted area *(see A in fig. 4)* and begin twisting wire again tightly for four rotations *(see fig. 5)*.

TIP *It's a good idea to do a little practice run with this project to get the twisting technique consistent. Don't worry if some of your twists are a little longer or shorter. This will add to the charm of the piece.*

MATERIALS

One spool 26-gauge silver beading wire

One small container silver seed beads

Thirteen 6 mm light pink freshwater pearls

Seventy-two 4 mm clear crystal beads

One three-holed silver clasp

Heavy-duty scissors for cutting wire

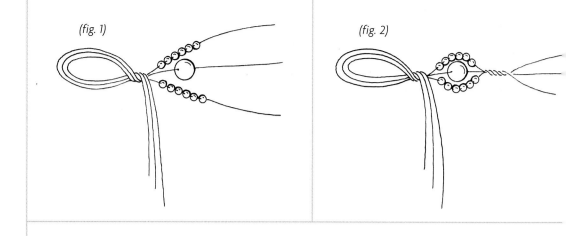

(fig. 1)   *(fig. 2)*

7. Add another 4 mm crystal onto the same wire. Repeat steps five and six two times until you have three 4 mm beads secured on the right wire.

8. Follow steps five to seven on the left wire until the arrangement of crystal beads looks like *fig. 6* with three beads on the right and left wires, no beads on the center wire.

9. Gather wires together at the bases of the twisted sections. Twist all three wires together tightly four rotations. Arrange the six wires with bead attachments until this section of the necklace forms a star *(see detail photo on facing page)*.

10. Repeat steps one through nine until you have thirteen sets of pearl beads framed by the silver seed beads and twelve sets of the star arrangement.

11. To finish off the piece, untwist beginning loop from step two. Twist wire ends of choker four times on each end. Add three silver seed beads to each of the wires and pull each wire through a hole on the clasp. (If the necklace fits a little large or small, add or subtract beads here for a proper fit.) Feed each loose wire end back through three seed beads and trim with heavy-duty scissors.

TIP *Choose beads that reflect the colors of your wedding material, whether that be bridesmaids' dresses, fiancé's accoutrements, or boutonniere.*

(fig. 3)

1/4"

(fig. 4)

A

(fig. 5)

(fig. 6)

Guided by Ancestors

Tradition is a funny thing. Some of us go out of our way to be free from it. Others are warmed by the prospect of continuing actions that originated generations before we were born. It links us to the past and to others who follow the same traditions.

How does that relate to weddings? Almost inextricably. In your everyday life, you are able to choose which traditions to perpetuate, stop, or initiate. However, it can be very difficult to remove a traditional element from a wedding. Why? Many people don't want to do anything that could sever their ties from peers or family, even if they don't like an element of the tradition. Oddly enough, it can be much easier to let our great grandparents make a decision about our wedding day than it is to make a decision of our own. With the stress that the weight of tradition brings, it's no wonder.

Tradition is precarious because it can be both helpful and restrictive. It forms a structure for you to wrap your experience around, which can help you immensely as you try to form a meaningful and memorable event. Tradition lets guests know what is coming and it lets you know what others expect of you. But it can also feel suffocating. If you like some traditional elements, but find others distasteful, it can be difficult to follow the ones you like and dispense with the others. How can you follow one tradition and reject another? The answer is simple: You just do. If you don't want to wear a white dress, then don't. Don't let history make that decision for you. Queen Victoria wore a white dress because she thought it was beautiful, not because everyone else wore one. Make your own choices.

Pay close attention to your thoughts as you contemplate changing, removing, or even elaborating traditions. Take care that you make every decision on purpose. Make sure every element of your wedding is what you want and what makes sense to you—not just what everyone in town does. That goes for all elements, traditional or not. If you want a three-tiered wedding cake just like everyone in your family has done for decades, make that decision because that is the cake you want, not because it is the one your family expects.

COMPROMISES

Every now and then (okay, every day) an iconoclast marries someone who values traditions. Learning how to communicate what you want, and learning to accept what someone else requires is nothing new to you. This is the perfect time to put that skill into full swing. If you're not the traditional type, you may have to learn to appreciate some traditions anyway. We know you'll be great at it.

THE CRAFT CONNECTION

What does tradition have to do with crafts? Plenty. Tradition affects the style of your wedding, what you do at the reception, and any number of things leading up to the wedding. Some of these controlling traditions may be cultural, others are familial. If every reception in the family has been a sit-down dinner, you probably feel comfortable following the same format. Crafts let you add your own stamp with unique centerpieces and a guest book that set your nuptials apart from anyone else's, regardless of the common features. Tradition is not a cookie-cutter, after all. It is an inspiration and a starting point. Use that inspiration to include meaningful elements that invoke your humor, wit, and style. ✳

Reception & Decor

A wedding is, essentially, a celebration with an official ceremony. The reception is a chance for your friends and family to celebrate your happiness and joy. It is also your opportunity to thank them for their love and support. Throw them a good party.

No matter what size the reception is, you know to cover the basics.

* Never leave your guests for long periods of time. Keep the photo sessions to a tight schedule and hustle the bustle. At one wedding we attended, we calculated that the bride and groom had only 4 minutes to spend with each guest! Don't waste time away from the people you've invited.

* Give people the right amount of food for the time of day. Serve food that you love to eat.

* Provide some entertainment in the form of music, dancing, or dining.
* Explain things. Many people choose their wedding activities from the same giant menu of traditions. If you are writing your own menu (bravo!), you may need to explain some elements that may be unfamiliar, either in a program or by announcement. Guests will feel most comfortable and ready to celebrate when they know what's going on.

A reception is more than a post-ceremony get-together. It is an experience, and you are in charge of the ambiance. Know which elements are important to you and which you want to let go. We believe you should pay some attention to the details and objects that people see, but the guests are the real focus. We feel pretty sure that the people you know are cool enough to take to the dance floor or make conversation, regardless of the details. What you want to do is encourage that natural liveliness and match the reception details to your personalities—so up the charm.

The reception should be comfortable and should contribute to your guests' experiences. This chapter is filled with ideas to enhance the party-half of the day. From centerpieces to favors, and card boxes to guest books, these projects give you ways to personalize your reception and live it up! Think through the event and imagine what people might want, how they might feel, and what they might need. If you approach it from their point of view and think about their enjoyment (as well as your own), you can't go wrong. What better way to celebrate the special day than by being perfect hosts together?

Hunka Burnin' Love

PHOTO VOTIVE

MATERIALS

Off-white pillar candle, about 6" (15.2 cm) high

Four to seven photo strips of you and your partner taken at a photo booth

8¹⁄₂" × 11" (21.6 cm × 27.9 cm) vellum

White inkjet or laser paper

Photocopier or printer and scanner

Glue stick

A great evening like this calls for some pretty special lighting. The soft, warm light of candles takes the edge off restaurant or ballroom lighting and creates intimate gatherings at each table. The glow of lightly fluttering flames softens surroundings and, let's face it, everyone looks great in a little candlelight. Rather than opt for plain candles, use pictures to make mini beacons of love. Since many guests may not have seen you and your sweetie in a while, these votives can help them feel as if they have been closer than geography may allow. When the wick is lit, the emanating light illuminates the vellum images wrapped around the candle.

1. Copy photo strips onto vellum. Either take the photos to a local copy center or scan them with your computer and print them on special inkjet- or laser-compatible vellum. Both color and black-and-white copies work well. Line up several of the photo strips across the copier or scanner bed. Butt the strips against each other so they are tight and parallel. The long edge of the photo strips should run across the short dimension of the paper.

2. Reduce the size of the photos so that the strip is the height of the candle: in the featured candle, 6" (15.2 cm). You will have to print two copies in order to cover the circumference of your candle, 11" (27.9 cm). Mesh the two pieces by overlapping by ¹⁄₈" (3 mm) of the nonprinted edges. (You might want to print up a trial run on regular paper.)

3. Wrap the paper around the candle pillar and trim so there is no more than ¹⁄₄" (6.4 mm) overlap.

4. Glue seams with a glue stick.

5. Place on a bed of uncooked rice in the center of each table.

VARIATION *Looking for a unique unity candle? Make a larger, taller version of this votive and use it during the ceremony. Simply use a 12" (30.5 cm) pillar candle. Enlarge the photos and print on a larger piece of vellum. Measure the circumference of the candle with a string to help you size the photos.*

The Ties That Bind

These Japanese-style photo albums are elegant and popular. There's a reason for that: they're lovely. They're also *très cher* in our favorite boutiques, where you'll soon see that the beauty translates rather swiftly into price, with numbers easily in excess of $90. Although this project is not easy, it is doable—and you can choose all the materials to fit your tastes instead of searching for a ready-made album to match your size requirements or style.

With projects that test the mettle of your craft skills, it is especially important to start well before the big day. In fact, it is important to finish it well before the wedding. Just set aside time to get it done (see "Budgeting Time" on page 30) and be realistic. Although we firmly believe that you must give yourself some leeway when it comes to schedules, you certainly don't want to return from your honeymoon with photos in hand and a half-assembled album to house them. Many wedding photos have languished in boxes in basements around the world for want of the perfect place to display them. (You wondered what was in those boxes, didn't you?) Should you leave the more complex projects to other people? Absolutely not! Items that you make for other people mean a lot because they are made by your own hands. Don't discount yourself—give yourself the best you can.

VARIATION *You can make these albums any size. To make the larger album in photo, we changed the dimensions to 16 ¼" x 13" (41.3 cm x 33 cm) and we didn't include the window. Simply make the height of the spine equal to the height of the cover board.*

MATERIALS FOR SMALLER ALBUM WITH WINDOW

Two sheets 13" × 20" (33 cm × 51 cm) book board

Two sheets of cream-colored 30" × 40" (76.2 cm × 101.6 cm) watercolor paper

Two sheets 20" × 30" (51 cm × 76.2 cm) decorative paper (hand block printed or wallpaper)

One sheet of book cloth

Utility knife

Craft knife

Bone folder

Manual or motorized drill

One 9/32" (7.1 mm) drill bit

C-clamps

One jar PVA glue

One bookbinder's brush

Metal ruler

Sharp pencil

Drafting triangle

3 yards (2.7 m) of 1/2" or 3/4" (1.3 cm or 1.9 cm) wide organdy or organza ribbon

Photo corners

Embroidery needle

Embroidery thread

Large newsprint tablet

White eraser

25" × 30" (63.5 cm × 76.2 cm) wooden board

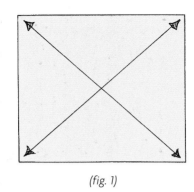

(fig. 1)

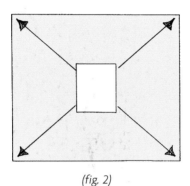

(fig. 2)

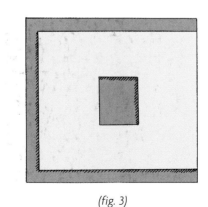

(fig. 3)

DIRECTIONS FOR SMALLER ALBUM

1. Measure two boards 12" wide x 10 ½" high (30.5 cm x 26.7 cm) with pencil and ruler. Use your triangle to square everything up, holding it against top and bottom edges to help you draw perpendicular lines in pencil.

2. On one of the 12" wide x 10 ½" high (30.5 cm x 26.7 cm) boards, draw diagonal lines from corner to corner *(see fig. 1)*. This will determine the center point of the front of the book.

3. Measure a rectangle 2" wide x 2 ½" high (5.1 cm x 6.4 cm) around the center point *(see fig. 2)*, making sure the rectangle is centered on the point (1 ¼" [3.2 cm] to the top and bottom of the center point, 1" [2.5 cm] to the left and right of the point). Draw the rectangle using your triangle to square things up.

4. On same boards, measure up two front spines, 2" wide x 10 ½" high (5.1 cm x 26.7 cm). Draw pencil lines for those.

5. Cut out boards with metal ruler and utility knife. Cut out window rectangle on front cover.

6. Measure and cut out two sheets of the decorative paper 13" wide x 12 ½" high (33 cm x 31.8 cm), making sure to square up the cuts against the paper's design, especially if it is geometric.

7. Lay paper decorative side down on a sheet of newsprint. Place front cover board on top of decorative paper, leaving 1" (2.5 cm) all around top, left, and bottom edges. The right edge should be flush with edge of decorative paper *(see fig. 3)*.

8. Brush a light coat of PVA glue onto wrong side of paper, making sure you cover the entire sheet. You will need to work fast because PVA glue sets up very quickly. (To slow the drying time, you may want to purchase some methyl cellulose and make a mixture of half methyl cellulose and half PVA.) Adhere paper to board and smooth out bubbles with edge of bone folder. Get out as many air bubbles as possible while doing this. It may look a little bumpy, but this should all smooth out as glue dries. You should burnish out as many wrinkles or major bumps as you can.

9. Using a craft knife on the paper corners, cut 45° angles on the top and bottom, and a square corner on the left edge corners *(see fig. 4)*.

10. Fold left edge of paper inward and burnish edge of book cover with bone folder. Brush on additional glue where needed and burnish flat. Do the same with the top and bottom edges.

11. With decorative paper face down on work surface, cut diagonals in front cover window *(see fig. 5)*. Brush on some glue and adhere to inside front cover. Burnish with bone folder.

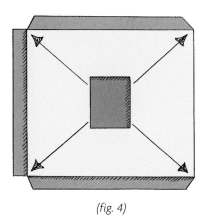

(fig. 4)

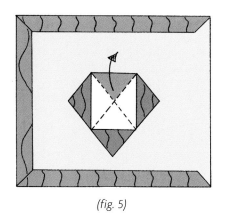

(fig. 5)

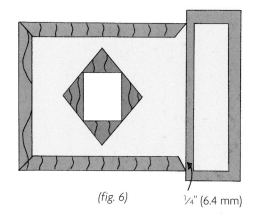

(fig. 6)   ¼" (6.4 mm)

12. For back cover, lay paper decorative side down on a sheet of newsprint. Place back cover board on top of decorative paper, leaving 1" (2.5 cm) all around top, right, and bottom edges. The left edge should be flush with edge of decorative paper.

13. Repeat step eight for back cover.

14. Using a craft knife on the paper corners, cut 45° angles on the top and bottom, and a square corner on the right edge corners *(mirror image of fig. 4)*.

15. Fold right edge of paper inward and burnish edge of book cover with bone folder. Brush on additional glue where needed and burnish flat. Do the same with the top and bottom edges.

16. For front and back spines, measure out two pieces 3 ¾" wide x 12 ½" high (9.5 cm x 31.8 cm) of bookbinding fabric. Square up with triangle and cut out the pieces.

17. On cover board, measure in ¾" (1.9 cm) from left and draw a vertical pencil line, squaring up line with triangle.

18. Butt book cloth against pencil line, leaving 1" (2.5 cm) on top and 1" (2.5 cm) on the bottom of fabric. Brush glue onto the fabric and glue into place. Burnish with bone folder, making sure not to stab fabric with the pointy end. Do not fold in top and bottom edges yet.

19. Lay book cover face down and place spine board to the right of it, leaving a ¼" (6.4 mm) gap between cover and spine *(see fig. 6)*. Make sure to leave the gap, otherwise the book cover will not open flat.

20. Brush glue onto the book cloth and adhere to spine board. Follow corner cutting technique discussed in step nine. Glue and burnish edges into inside front cover.

21. Attach a back spine board. On back cover board, measure in ¾" (1.9 cm) from right and draw a vertical pencil line, squaring up line with triangle.

glue flap to itself

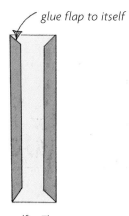

(fig. 7)

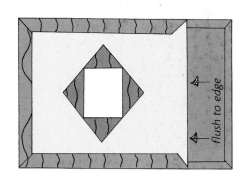

flush to edge

(fig. 8)

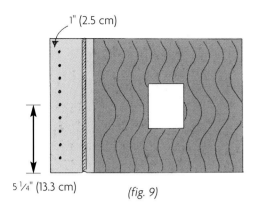

1" (2.5 cm)

5 ¼" (13.3 cm)

(fig. 9)

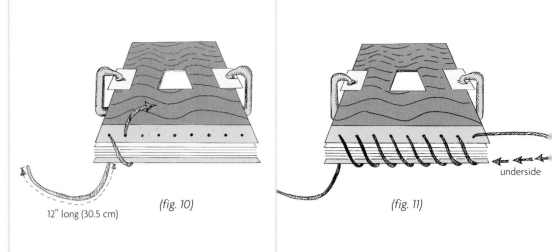

12" long (30.5 cm)

(fig. 10)

underside

(fig. 11)

22. Butt the book cloth against pencil line, leaving 1" (2.5 cm) on top and 1" (2.5 cm) on the bottom of the fabric. Brush some glue onto the fabric and glue into place. Burnish with bone folder, making sure not to stab fabric with the pointy end. Do not fold in top and bottom edges yet.

23. Lay book cover face down and place spine to the left of it, leaving a ¼" (6.4 mm) gap between cover and spine.

24. Brush glue onto the bookbinding fabric and adhere to spine. Follow corner cutting technique discussed in step nine. Glue and burnish edges into inside front cover. Using point of bone folder, push fabric down into the gaps between spines and covers.

25. For spine end papers, cut two 2 ½" x 10 ½" (6.4 cm x 26.7 cm) rectangles out of the book cloth. Fold fabric in ½" (1.3 cm) on the top and bottom and glue to fabric itself *(see fig. 7)*. Lay book cover decorative side down. Butt fabric against inner edge of binding fabric, leaving ½" (1.3 cm) top and bottom. Glue into place and burnish *(see fig. 8)*.

26. Repeat process for back spine end paper.

27. For endsheets, cut out 11 ¾" wide x 10" high (29.8 cm x 25.4 cm) sheet of decorative paper for the inside cover. Lay one sheet decorative side up on inside front cover. Flip board over and raw a pencil outline of the window. Cut out window. Brush on glue and place ¼" (6.4 mm) in from top, bottom, and left edges and flush with right cover edge, making sure paper window aligns with cardboard cover window. Repeat process for back inside cover, leaving off the window step.

28. For inside pages, measure ten 10" x 14" (25.4 cm x 35.6 cm) sheets of watercolor paper. Mark *very lightly* with a pencil. Place the metal ruler to the left of pencil line as you would if you were going to trim out the pages with a craft knife. Instead, put pressure on your ruler with your left hand. With your right hand tear the page along the ruler edge from top to bottom, forming a deckled edge. Erase any visible pencil lines with a white eraser.

29. Stack and straighten pages as best you can and place in book, centering from top to bottom, but running flush with spine.

30. Measure and draw a vertical pencil line 1" (2.5 cm) in from the left edge of your cover. Make a tick mark at the vertical center of that line, at 5 1/4" (13.3 cm). Make four tick marks to the bottom of the center point, 1 1/8" (2.9 cm) apart. Then make four tick marks to the top of the center point, 1 1/8" (2.9 cm) apart, for a total of nine tick marks *(see fig. 9)*.

31. Straighten the pages and cover, and C-clamp the spine of book onto the edge of a wooden board. You may want to place a piece of paper or cardboard between your clamps and your cover to protect the paper.

32. Drill holes at each of the tick marks, going straight through all the layers of the book and through the back cover. Unclamp and erase pencil line with a white eraser.

33. Take 3 yards (2.7 m) of ribbon and sew on a 6" (15.2 cm) length of thread to the end. Start sewing book binding as follows: Starting at hole one, run ribbon through the bottom of book and out through the top of hole one leaving 12" (30.5 cm) of ribbon hanging off end. Wrap ribbon around spine and proceed up through hole two *(see fig. 10)*. Repeat this process through all the holes until you've come to hole nine. At that point, wrap ribbon around outside of the bottom of the spine to underside of hole nine *(see fig. 11)*. Pass the needle and ribbon up through *(see fig. 12)*. While you do this, make sure you do not split the ribbon that is already in the hole. Splitting the ribbon can happen easily, but can be avoided by pulling the ribbon currently in the hole to the side as you pass the needle and ribbon through a second time. Wrap the ribbon over the spine, forming a criss-cross with the ribbon that has already been sewn. Proceed to the underside of hole eight, pulling the ribbon up through hole eight *(see fig. 13)*. Continue this same process through all the holes until you are back at hole one. Wrap remaining ribbon around top of the spine and tie the two ends in a bow *(see fig. 14)*.

34. Trim ends of ribbon by folding vertically in half and cutting a 45° angle. This will give your ends a dart in the middle.

35. Place photos in book with photo corners.

T I P *Keep a kitchen towel handy during this project. When burnishing the bubbles and wrinkles out of the paper, glue can seep from the seams. Use the towel to wipe up the excess glue immediately to prevent damaging the decorative paper.*

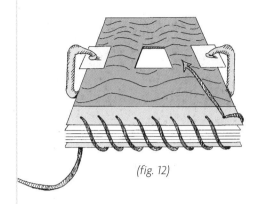

(fig. 12)

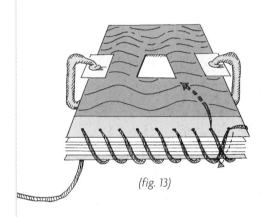

(fig. 13)

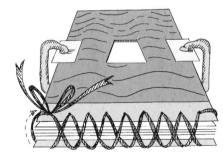

(fig. 14)

Zen Centerpiece

SLEEK BAMBOO GARDEN

MATERIALS

One shallow square dish

Heavy metal flower frog

Three protea flowers

Seven tall, curly fresh bamboo stems

Gardening shears

Gray river pebbles, enough to cover the bottom of the dish and the metal frog

A miniature forest of green bamboo on each table creates a sleek and serene décor that projects a modern simplicity. By using only two types of plants set in a shallow bowl of glossy river stones, you manufacture a relaxing and lush table setting. Curly bamboo is long lasting and fast growing. The tall stalks have fantastic coils in the stems and satiny dark green leaves that add a mild texture to the centerpiece. It takes some force to settle the stems into a metal frog, but once in place and watered, they will last for a long time, and certainly won't wilt during the day or evening. The centerpiece should not block guests' view, so place it judiciously, or make a version people can peer over.

1. Cut the bottoms of the curly bamboo down to about 24" (61 cm), varying the heights slightly to fit the curly gnarls into one another.

2. Place the bamboo into the center of the frog. Secure to frog by piercing the bottom of the stems with the needles of the frog.

3. Cut the bottoms of the protea, and score the bottom edges of the stems with the shears, so they fit into the frog needles. Place on the outside edges of the frog around the bamboo.

4. Fill the dish with rocks, covering the frog and the bottom. Fill with water.

TIP *If you have a difficult time settling the bamboo stalks into a metal frog, pierce the bottom of the stalk with a small nail. Don't make a big hole, just an indention to guide the frog points.*

Natural sugar
(sandy color)

Two interior
gardening pebbles

One sheet $1/8$" (3 mm)
thick balsa wood, cut
down to 4" wide × 6"
high (10.2 cm × 15.2 cm)

One strip of
$1/2$" × $1/2$"
(1.3 cm × 1.3 cm)
balsa wood

Black semigloss
latex paint

Small paintbrush

Mitre box

Small saw

Wood glue

Small rattan rake

Ruler

Drafting triangle, 45°

Pencil

Sandpaper

Wood filler

A Garden of One's Own

ZEN ROCK GARDEN

Is the food too good to play with during dinner? Perhaps there's a long time between courses. A Zen rock garden is the toy for fidgety fingers or pauses in conversation. Every time you rake the surface, you create a new work of art. We filled our gardens with natural, unbleached sugar, so it looks like sand, but won't be gritty if a little winds up in the food. (And you can't guarantee against that when there is champagne to be had.) Set one garden at each place setting, or place one between settings, so people share the Zen experience. Rake the surface and place the pebbles before guests arrive. A perfect accompaniment to the Zen bamboo garden (see page 98), pair these decorations with a bamboo placemat, sand-colored dishes, and chopsticks.

1. Measure two strips of the ½" x ½" (1.3 cm x 1.3 cm) balsa wood to 6" (15.2 cm). Place a tick mark with pencil at 6" (15.2 cm). With the triangle, draw a line 45° inward from the 6" (15.2 cm) tick mark. Do this on both ends. Place in mitre box and cut, leaving a small allowance for the saw blade.

2. Measure two strips of the ½" x ½" (1.3 cm x 1.3 cm) balsa wood to 4" (10.2 cm). Place a tick mark with pencil at 4" (10.2 cm). With the triangle, draw a line 45° inward from the 4" (10.2 cm) tick mark. Do this on both ends. Place in mitre box and cut, once again leaving a small allowance for the saw blade.

3. Place 4" (10.2 cm) pieces and 6" (15.2 cm) pieces on top of the ⅛" x 4" x 6" (3 mm x 10.2 cm x 15.2 cm) rectangle you cut in step one, creating a framework around the outer edges.

4. Make sure mitred edges fit together nicely, you may have to do a little sanding to make them meet exactly.

5. Glue framework onto 4" x 6" (10.2 cm x 15.2 cm) base and let glue set about 20 minutes.

6. Fill any cracks with wood filler and let that set about ½ hour.

7. Sand lightly to remove any extra wood filler or rough edges on balsa wood.

8. Paint it black and let it dry 1 hour.

9. Fill with natural sugar and rocks.

10. Make a design around the rocks with either the rake or a pencil.

11. Place rake in the sugar-sand and place the garden on the table.

VARIATION *The mini garden can double as a place card holder. Print out the names, and nestle them into the sugar-sand. But if you prefer the rock garden to be amusing instead of useful, use silk "fortune cookies" as place cards. Write each name on a scroll of paper and place in the cookie.*

Toying with Guests

Normally place cards don't move. These do…when you wind them up and let them loose on the table. In a sly reference to formal wear, wind-up penguins or monkeys are an amusing and charming injection of fun. A kitsch element like a wind-up toy relies on the guests' knowledge of your personality and humor. If everyone thinks of you as the epitome of refinement—whether correct or not—they may think the style doesn't quite match. However, if your style is relaxed and modern, these toys will be a huge hit.

DIRECTIONS FOR THE MONKEY GIRLS

1. Cut a 3" (7.6 cm) strip of faux pearl ribbon. Shape pearls around head of monkey. Glue into place using the cotton swabs.

2. Trim off row of pearls from back of veil. Add a daisy to the hand and wrap wire at least two times around wrist of monkey. Secure wire end and cut with scissors.

3. Use your favorite computer layout software to inset each guest name in an oval $3/4$" wide x $1/2$" high (1.9 cm x 1.3 cm). For a decorative element, you can add a tilde underneath the name.

4. Print the names.

5. Cut out the ovals and dab a little glue on the back of the paper. Adhere to belly of the monkey girl.

VARIATION *For a slightly different look along the same lines, use different wind-up creatures. Frogs will give a funnier look to a place setting. Robots will give a futuristic look.*

MATERIALS

Miniature wind up toys, about 2" tall (5.1 cm)

Personal computer

Printer

Your favorite computer layout software

Bright white inkjet or laser paper

Guest list

$1/4$" (6.4 mm) black ribbon

2" (5.1 cm) translucent wire ribbon with faux pearls on edges

Party favor daisies

Roundstone sequins

PVA or craft glue

Cotton swabs

Scissors

DIRECTIONS FOR THE MONKEY BOYS

1. Cut an 8" (20.3 cm) strip of black ribbon. Tie a bow around the monkey neck. Trim ends on a diagonal with scissors.

2. Glue a roundstone sequin to each of the monkey ears.

3. Repeat step three and four from the monkey girl directions.

4. Cut out the ovals with scissors and dab a little glue on the back. Adhere to belly of the monkey boy.

DIRECTIONS FOR THE EMPIRE PENGUIN GIRLS

1. Cut a 3" (7.6 cm) strip of faux pearl ribbon. Shape pearls around head of penguin. Glue into place using the cotton swabs.

2. Trim off row of pearls from back of veil. Add two roundstone sequins vertically about $\frac{1}{4}$" (6.4 mm) under penguin girl's beak.

3. Use your favorite computer layout software to inset each guest name in a rectangle $\frac{3}{4}$" wide x $\frac{1}{2}$" high (1.9 cm x 1.3 cm). We used 9 point Bernhard Tango typeface for ours. For a decorative element, you can add a tilde underneath the name.

4. Print the names.

5. Cut out the rectangles with scissors and dab a little glue on the back. We cut a little diagonal in the name card to make it look like it was going under her arm. Adhere next to the wing of the penguin girl.

DIRECTIONS FOR THE EMPIRE PENGUIN BOYS

1. Cut an 8" (20.3 cm) strip of black ribbon. Tie a bow around the penguin neck. Trim ends on a diagonal with scissors.

2. Using a cotton swab, glue two roundstone sequins vertically under the bow tie.

3. Use your favorite computer layout software to inset each guest name in a rectangle $\frac{3}{4}$" wide x $\frac{1}{2}$" high (1.9 cm x 1.3 cm). We used 9 point Bernhard Tango typeface for ours. For a decorative element, you can add a tilde underneath the name.

4. Print the names.

5. Cut out the rectangles with scissors and dab a little glue on the back. We cut a little diagonal in the name card to make it look like it was going under his arm. Adhere to the wing of the penguin boy.

MATERIALS

8" (20.3 cm), 11" (27.9 cm),
14" (35.6 cm) hatboxes

Six sheets of 20" × 30"
(50.8 cm × 76.2 cm)
decorative paper
(allow two sheets
for each tier)

Spray adhesive

Craft knife

Bone folder

Daisy combo packet of
rubber flowers

Black-and-white
photocopy of a couple
in wedding attire

Black-and-white
photocopy of you and
your spouse's faces
to fit onto wedding
couple image

8" × 10 1/4"
(20.3 cm × 26 cm)
black foam core

Small paper flowers
for party favors

One box
roundstone sequins

One packet
rhinestones
1/2" (1.3 cm) and
5/8" (1.6 cm)

1/2 yard (.5 m)
netting or tulle

Craft glue

Pencil

Tiers of Joy
WEDDING CAKE CARD BOX

Card boxes are not a necessity, but many couples use them to assure that cards and messages stay together and safe. Because guests do not always bring gifts and cards to a reception, it is a good idea to place a card box, or indeed a gift table, in a non-prominent position. Even though you don't want gifts to take center stage, you can still go vivid. Think outside the box — or at least re-shape it — and appropriate a standard image for a different purpose.

1. Top tier: Take off lid of 8" (20.3 cm) hatbox (the lid will not be used in the final project). Trace around lid shape onto back side of top tier paper. Start cutting, leaving about 3/4" (1.9 cm) extra all around as you cut. Final circle size should be around 9" (22.9 cm) in diameter.

2. Spray adhesive onto back of circle and center on bottom of 8" (20.3 cm) hatbox. Smooth out bumps with a bone folder. Press extra paper over edges and smooth with bone folder, flattening as best you can the small creases that happen as the paper wraps around the circular shape. Flip the box bottom side up. This will now be the top of the cake.

3. Measure the depth of the sides of the circular box. The top tier shown measured 3 1/2" (8.9 cm). Add 3/4" (1.9 cm) to the depth, to allow enough paper to tuck to the inside of the box. Cut that dimension out of the second piece of paper along the entire length of the paper.

VARIATION *If your wedding will be more traditional than funky, look for papers, or even fabrics, that match your style. Remnants of silk georgette with accents of lace look very beautiful in the cake form. You can also find inexpensive buttons and hot glue them to the box, making Victorian stylized flower clusters.*

Ours was 4 ¼" x 30" (10.8 cm x 76.2 cm). Spray adhesive on the back side of the paper and adhere it to the box, butting the paper edge against the top of the "cake" and tucking the extra ³⁄₄" (1.9 cm) of paper into the inside of the box. Smooth with bone folder.

4. Middle tier: Select second tier paper style. Take the lid off the 11" (27.9 cm) hatbox. Discard the lid. Follow the instructions for top tier, measuring the depth of the sides and adding ³⁄₄" (1.9 cm) extra for tucking in edges. If paper does not make the circumference of the box, add another strip, matching design as best you can.

5. Bottom tier: Take the lid off the 14" (35.6 cm) hatbox. Keep the lid. Cut a 6 ³⁄₄" x ¼" (17.1 cm x 6.4 mm) slit 1 ¼" (3.2 cm) in from the edge of the lid. This will be the slit for the cards. Place a sheet of decorative paper on the work surface, right side down. Place the lid on top and trace around it with a pencil. Cut out the shape, leaving a ³⁄₄" (1.9 cm) allowance all around. Spray adhesive onto the back side of the paper and cover top of hatbox lid, tucking the ³⁄₄" (1.9 cm) extra over the lid edge. Burnish with bone folder. Flip lid over and cut out paper from slit with a craft knife.

6. Measure depth of lid side and then add ³⁄₄" (1.9 cm) to tuck under the rim. Cut out strip and spray mount to lid side, butting top edge of paper against top edge of lid. Fold extra paper to underside of lid and burnish. If the paper is not big enough to cover the entire circumference of the box, add another strip, matching the design as best you can.

7. Measure depth of box. This time add 1 ½" (3.8 cm) extra to depth for folding inside box and onto bottom. Spray adhesive to the underside of the paper and burnish onto the side of the box, leaving ³⁄₄" (1.9 cm) to fold over the top of the box and ³⁄₄" (1.9 cm) on the bottom. Burnish with bone folder, folding in top edges and folding under bottom edges.

8. Place the lid on the bottom tier.

9. When decorating the box, you can do just about anything you want. We followed the concept of a traditional cake, but made it livelier to match the colorful pattern. We pasted the little flowers around the top tier and then glued the ½" (1.3 cm) rhinestones to the flower centers. Paste roundstones on a glue strip arc forming swags around the cake.

10. Because the second tier is larger than the top, use bigger flowers and the ³/₄" (1.9 cm) rhinestones in the center of the flowers. Repeat the roundstone swags of the first tier and make edging around the top and bottom of this tier with the roundstone sequins. Paste rhinestones around the paper. In our example, we placed them in the bottom squares of the tier.

11. Use the biggest flowers on the third tier and glue the ³/₄" (1.9 cm) rhinestones in the center of each flower. In the example shown, we glued the decorations to the lid. Glue roundstones in swags around the tier.

12. For the bride and groom, spray mount the bride and groom image to a piece of foam core. Cut out the shape of couple. Leave about ½" (1.3 cm) strip at their feet. Make sure the strip is square, so the bride and groom will stand up straight, not leaning to one side. Measure the width of the base of the bride and groom. Add ½" (1.3 cm) to that dimension and cut out a strip of foam core that long by 1" (2.5 cm) high. Out of the center of that strip, cut a channel ¼" (6.4 mm) high by the width of the bride and groom figure. Insert bride and groom feet first into the stand and adhere together with craft glue.

13. With pencil point, stab a hole in the bride's hands where the bouquet will be. Place three paper flowers in the hole and pull the wires through to the back of foam core. Twist wire so flowers don't fall out.

14. Obviously, you won't have any wedding pictures of yourselves at this point. Cut out the faces of the black-and-white photocopies of you and your fiancé. Glue them to the wedding portrait. Add a few roundstone sequins to the headpiece and glue the bride and groom to the top tier of the cake.

15. Glue the three tiers together at each of the bases. Top with a 26" (66 cm) piece of netting folded in half to 13" (33 cm). You can secure this by placing a few straight pins through the netting into the heads of the bride and groom.

TIP *One strip of paper may not be enough to cover each hatbox. You may need to use extra strips of paper and match up the design.*

Chapel of Love

SACRED TABLE TOPPER

There's something satisfying about appropriating a standard *Saturday Evening Post* image for decorative purposes. A chapel in a field and a couple speeding away in a "Just Married" convertible recall an archetype of love and marriage. It becomes half humor and half homage. More often than not, reality looks very different from this idyllic image. That's really part of the fun. If you were getting married in a country chapel and speeding away in a convertible, this centerpiece would seem oddly self-referential. But, for other styles of weddings, this centerpiece is amusing and calls up the idea of a wedding in general and the free feeling of speeding away with your sweetheart.

1. Place 11" x 11" (27.9 cm x 27.9 cm) piece of faux grass directly on top of 11" x 11" (27.9 cm x 27.9 cm) square of floral styrofoam.

2. Make a hole under the grass, about 3" (7.6 cm) from what will be the back and 5 ½" (14 cm) from the left of the square. Place the cord for the wreath lights through the hole. Lift up grass and run the cord of the wreath lights under the grass and out what will become the back of the centerpiece. Leave about 6" (15.2 cm) of cord with the batteries hanging out of the back of the piece.

TIP *Real sod and real flowers can be substituted for the faux grass and party favor daisies. The picket fences can be painted white before assembling. If there are any bald spots in the real grass, add 2" (5.1 cm) of floral wire into the hole and attach one of the sprigs you've removed to make room for the church.*

MATERIALS

11" × 11" × 1 ½" thick (27.9 cm × 27.9 cm × 3.8 cm) piece of floral styrofoam

Six pieces 5 ½" wide × 4 ½" high (14 cm × 11.4 cm) dollhouse fencing

11" × 11" (27.9 cm × 27.9 cm) square of faux grass

Fifteen party favor daisies

One 8 ½" × 11" (21.6 cm × 27.9 cm) piece of black craft foam sheeting

One scale train accessory model church

One scale train accessory bride and groom

One matchbox-size convertible car

One battery-operated set of wreath lights

2 yards (1.8 m) of 1 ½" wide (3.8 cm) lime green cotton ribbon

Small glass votive holder

Wood glue

Superglue

Floral wire

Fifteen to twenty medium-sized household nails

Personal computer and printer (optional)

Utility knife

Ruler

Drafting triangle

Two straight pins or needles and lime green thread

3. Measure and cut fencing to run around three sides of square foam and grass, making sure edges of fencing butt against each other closely. Weave floral wire in and out of the bottom of the fencing uprights.

4. Secure fencing and wire to styrofoam by pushing household nails through the woven wire into the styrofoam. Do this all around the bottom of the fencing until it feels tight and secure.

5. Glue the butted edges of the fence with wood glue.

6. Measure and cut a 2 ½" wide x 7 ½" long (6.4 cm x 19.1 cm) strip of black craft foam. This will be your road.

7. Clear a path for the road by pulling out some grass sprigs. Start at center front of centerpiece and work your way to back of square until you have cleared a path approximately 2 ½" wide x 6" long (6.4 cm x 15.2 cm).

8. Place your road on the centerpiece, leaving approximately 1 ½" (3.8 cm) protruding in front.

9. Wrap a ribbon all the way around the edges of the styrofoam bottom, starting and ending at center back. Cut the ribbon, leaving ½" (1.3 cm) extra to tuck under. Tuck under edge and secure to styrofoam using the straight pins. (You could also handstitch this if you want.)

10. Tuck protruding part of road under ribbon in front.

11. Assemble church model using instructions in kit, but don't mount it to base provided in kit.

12. Temporarily place the church at the end of the road. Pull out sprigs of grass to accommodate the base of the church, because you'll want the church to be nestled in the grass. Set the church aside.

13. Stuff wreath lights into votive holder. Turn votive holder upside down and place in the nesting place you've just created for the church.

14. Place church on top of votive and nestle it into the grass.

15. Cut figurines of wedding couple in half with utility knife, so they sit nicely in the car. Superglue into place.

16. Using your favorite computer layout software, make a miniature "Just Married" sign to place on the back of the car. Print out the sign. Cut out and glue onto back of car.

17. Place car on road.

18. Place party favor daisies randomly on grass and stick stems through styrofoam.

19. Place batteries in wreath lights, turn on the switch, and watch your church glow.

Sticky Guest Book

MATERIALS

Personal computer

Your favorite computer layout software

Printer

Bright white inkjet or laser paper

Light pink inkjet or laser paper

Spray mount adhesive

Cellophane tape

Corrugated, wavy silver paper

Silver cord with tassels

iZone camera and adhesive film

Drafting triangle, 45°

Metal ruler

Bone folder

Craft knife

Template from page 125

Let's face it: guest books can be beautiful, but dead boring. Sorry, it's true. Liven it up a little and let your favorite people's creativity show with mini guest books on each table. Leave a booklet, an iZone camera, sticky film, and scissors on the table. Your guests are sure to take the most charming photos of each other living it up in celebration of you two. Instead of empty pages, give guests a head start with a rectangle to frame each photo and lines for the message. (After the third toast of the evening, lines will be helpful, indeed.)

1. Using your favorite computer layout software, create a document 4 ½" wide x 10" tall (11.4 cm x 25.4 cm). On one-half of the document, create a bordered box that measures 1 ½" wide x 1 ⅛" high (3.8 cm x 2.9 cm). Put the words "Place picture here" in the center of the box. Under the box, make several horizontal rules and some type that reads, "Wishes for the couple." Copy this layout onto the other half of the document and print it. Print six copies of this and trim to size.

2. Spray mount two of the sheets back to back until you have three back-to-back sheets. Fold sheets in half width-wise. Unfold and stack the sheets, so they will nest in each other when folded.

3. Create another page with the same dimensions and set some type that reads, "Guests," 2" (5.1 cm) from the top of the page and centered on one-half of the document on the right-hand side. Print on the light pink paper and trim. Fold in half and score with bone folder. Place in front of pages created in step one, so it will make the first and last pages of the book.

4. Photocopy the template from page 125 and tape on three sides to the back of the corrugated paper. Cut along straight lines and score along dotted lines. Cut out front window.

5. Using the bone folder, fold cover in half along score lines.

6. Place interior pages in book and tie into place with silver cord. Make a knot on the outside of book on the center of the spine.

7. Place one at each table with an iZone Polaroid camera, extra sticky film, scissors, and a pen.

Kiddie Confections

LOLLIPOP BOUQUET

Kids need a little extra fun at weddings. With all the adults gabbing and dancing, kids have a tendency to feel left out or restless. Keeping the younger guests happy and entertained keeps everyone else happy. A lollipop bouquet makes children part of the wedding itself, by taking a standard wedding icon and making it fun—that is, full of sugar. Yes, the sweets will enhance any hyperactivity, but if the adults are imbibing in their vices, why can't the kids? If you want a dramatic look, bundle a bunch of red lollipops in a lace collar. Ours reflects a garden theme, with silk leaves and marzipan fruits.

1. Attach 2" (5.1 cm) of floral wire to the end of each lollipop stick, wrapping it onto stick with white floral tape. Round out the lollipop wrappers with scalloped-edged scissors. Pierce popsicle sticks into back side of marzipan. Don't push sticks all the way through the candy.

2. Create a bouquet with the eight silk leaves, assembling them in a circle. Place all the lollipops and pinwheels into the center of the leaves in this order: three big lollipops in the back, four rectangular lollipops in the middle, three marzipan fruits in front, and two pinwheels on the right-hand side. Place two more rectangular lollipops behind the three large lollipops in the back to round out the bouquet.

3. Wrap base of stems with floral wire or floral tape to secure bouquet, if needed. Wrap the ribbon around the stems. Wrap the stems with enough ribbon to hide the floral wire and tape and tie off the end. Knot ribbon or wrap decoratively.

4. We placed the end of the ribbon below the calla lily leaves. Wrap the ribbon over the end of the stems and up the opposite side. Wrap ribbon around the stem, all the way down to the end. The stem should be covered. Knot ribbon or wrap decoratively.

5. With the ribbon in front, flip the ribbon up at an angle, exposing the reverse color and anchoring the ribbon in place with Superglue. Leave time for it to dry before flipping the ribbon back on itself, still in an upward angle. Anchor again. Trim end at an angle.

TIP *Use Saf-T-Pops for little kids if you worry that they will run around with lollipops in their mouths. For older kids, you can use dulled pins to hold the ribbon, otherwise, use Superglue.*

MATERIALS

Three pieces of marzipan fruits

Six multicolored rectangular lollipops

Three big round multicolored lollipops

Eight silk calla lily leaves

One roll of two-sided ribbon

Three popsicle sticks

Toys, like the pinwheels we used here

White floral tape

Green floral wire

Dulled straight pins

Superglue

Scalloped-edged decorative scissors

Where Do I Sit?

MATERIALS FOR TABLE ASSIGNMENT

Miniature dollhouse tables

Miniature dollhouse chairs

Personal computer and printer

Your favorite computer layout software

8 ½" × 11" (21.6 cm × 27.9 cm) colored stationery paper

Letter and number beads

Decorative beads

Tacks or brads

Beading wire

Bone folder

Craft knife

There's always a bit of excitement at the beginning of a reception when guests discover who their tablemates are. It's not uncommon to see calligraphied posters beautifully directing people to their appointed positions. Beautiful handwriting is one option; smart imagery is another. These miniature tables and chairs direct people in a charming and amusing way. Atop each miniature table, place a folded card listing the guests that will sit together at one table. Arrange the miniatures on the seat assignment table. Mark each person's position at their actual tables with their name resting on a miniature chair.

DIRECTIONS FOR TABLE ASSIGNMENT

1. Using your favorite computer layout software, create a 3" (7.6 cm) square for each table. Set the guests' names for each table in the bottom half of the squares. (The cards will be folded so you will only see part of each card).

2. Print onto your stationery paper and trim to size. Fold in half and score with bone folder.

3. String up three beads on your wire and then add letter beads to spell "TABLE 1," "TABLE 2," and so on. Place a single bead between "TABLE" and the number. Follow with three beads.

4. Hammer a brad into the underside of the left and right ends of front edge of table. Wrap the wire around brads and string along front.

5. Place card on table top. Place each card-topped miniature on the seating assignment table.

DIRECTIONS FOR SEATING ASSIGNMENT

1. Using your favorite computer layout software, create a 1 ½" high x 1 ¼" wide (3.8 cm x 3.2 cm) square for each chair. Set each guest's name in the bottom half of the square, one name to a square. (The cards will be folded so you will only read the bottom part of each card). Print and trim.

2. Fold in half and score with bone folder. Place each card on a miniature chair. Place the card-topped chair on each plate or at the head of each plate in dining area.

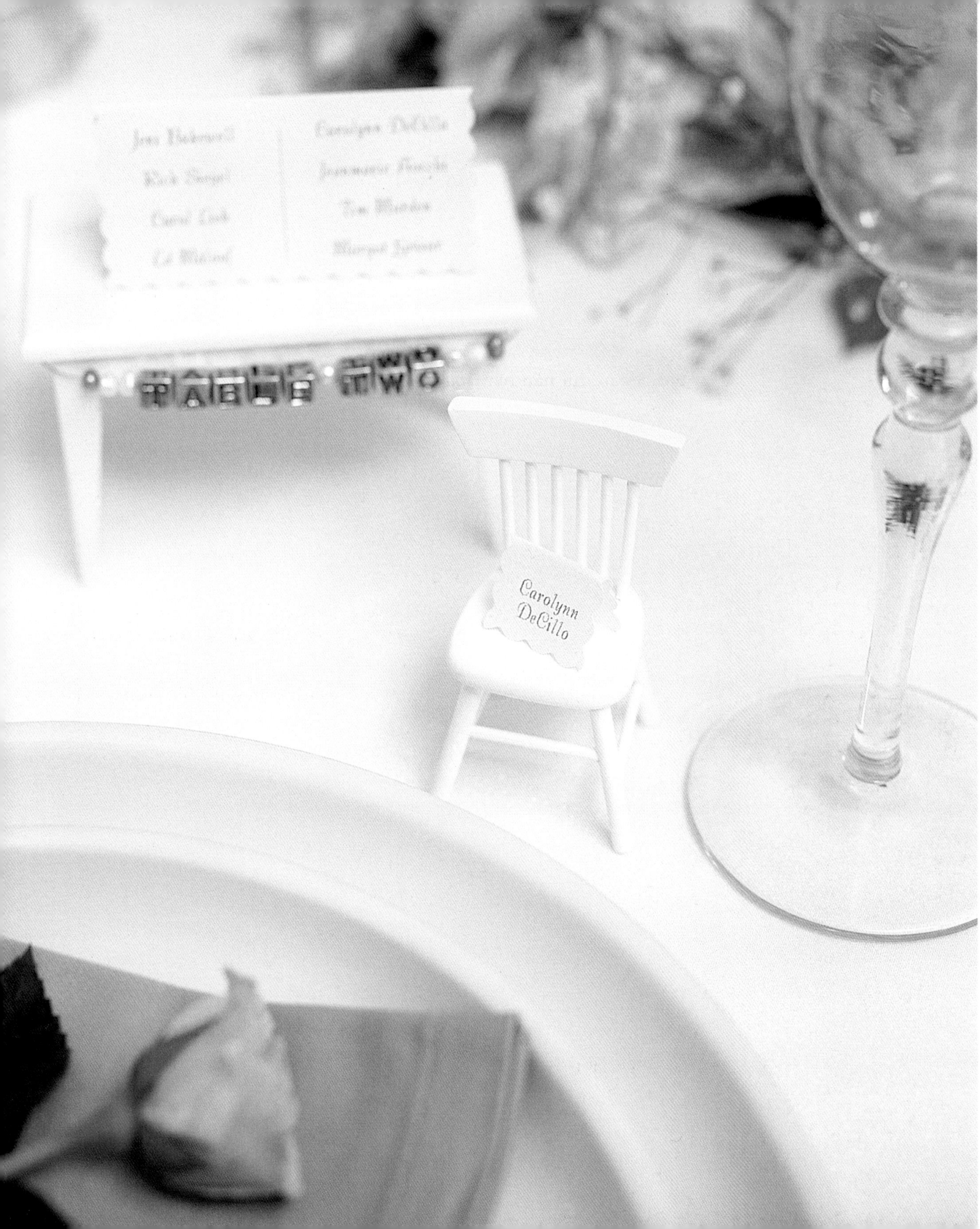
TABLE TWO
Carolynn DeCillo

Mini Frame To Go

PLACE CARD FRAME IN ORGANDY SACK

Place cards don't have to be disposable. A small frame with its own organdy sack serves as a beautiful place card during the reception. By dressing up a basic metal frame and with a little decoration, you provide a nice keepsake of the day. A small organdy sack not only ties the look into the rest of the décor, but makes it a take-away treasure.

Small, inexpensive frames and organdy bags can be found in most craft or card stores. If you have a prominent color scheme, buy the bags and decorations in both colors. Use one color for the roundstone sequins and the opposite color for the sack. If you don't want to over-coordinate, use the same color for both elements, for a subtler look.

1. With your favorite computer layout software, create a document that is 3 $\frac{1}{4}$" wide x 2 $\frac{1}{4}$" high (8.3 cm x 5.7 cm). You can also set up eight of these in an 8 $\frac{1}{4}$" x 11" (21 cm x 27.9 cm) document, two across and four down.

2. Type in guest's name, set in your favorite typeface, and center on page.

3. Print on colored stationery paper.

4. Cut out and insert in frame.

5. Glue roundstones on frame corners.

6. Place bag on plate or at the head of the place setting. Then place frame on bag. Guests can take the frames home in the little sacks.

VARIATION *Instead of printing guests' names, you can add a special touch with calligraphy. You can hire a calligrapher to make up the cards. Double-check the spelling of the guests' names before you give the artist the list and after the cards have been finished.*

MATERIALS

3" × 4" (7.6 cm × 10.2 cm) brushed silver frames

Purple roundstone sequins

Superglue

Craft knife

Printer

Personal computer

Your favorite computer layout software

Colored stationery paper

Organdy drawstring sack

Crafty Ways of Finding Help

When you're planning a wedding, or indeed anything, you're bound to hear your friends say, "Let me know if I can do anything to help." Let's face it, it's a basic tenet of friendship to offer help. That's how it should be. But that doesn't make it easy to call in the offer, and it certainly doesn't mean that a friend is willing to drop regular tasks, habits, or schedules to do whatever you ask. Asking for help is a craft in itself. Here's how to co-opt some friends into getting the projects done.

Photo: Ryan McVay, PictureQuest

1. First, let's decipher the offer. No matter how many fingers you cross, it does not mean that your friend will do anything. It's really an offer to listen to what you need to do, and muck in if it works out. If you think of something that might fit your friend's life or schedule, you should ask politely and with respect, even if she is your closest pal. After all, hip brides like you have a lot going on in their lives besides the wedding (that's part of what makes you hip), so it should be easy to understand the constraints on your friends' lives.

2. Most of your friends have heard about your plans and what sort of an event you and your main squeeze are planning. That makes the next step super-easy: Tell your friends what elements you are hoping to make and invite them to a craft party. The idea is to make an event for them, entertain them with company and food while the project assembly line goes into motion. Do anything you can to make it special, so your friends know you are asking not only for their help, but also their camaraderie.

Doubtless some friends do not feel handy and may be worried that they will ruin the projects. Tell them you have a couple of steps that are impossible to mess up that they can help with, and that they should come anyway for the fun and the champagne. (They will come and, before you know it, they will have mastered the simple project elements—they're not very difficult.) If that doesn't convince them, let them know that they can just hang out and quality check the goods—and the munchies. After all, even though you're making crafts, it's still a party and you want your friends to have a blast.

3. Make a couple examples of each project so you understand all the steps and can easily teach it to the others. Pay attention to where trouble might arise so you can lend an extra hand. Get all the supplies set up and separated by project, so no one will confuse the epoxy for one project with the binding glue for another. If certain materials need to be printed or photocopied, make sure you do that before the guests arrive. Make sure you have enough extras to cover any learning curve mistakes or demos.

4. Chill the champagne, pop the frozen hors d'oeuvres in the oven, get some great cheese and bread, and the best cookies you can find. Put the tunes on the stereo (we've found that Stereolab or the Bee Gees works best for us) and let people in the door. Make sure you have plenty of napkins.

5. Show people the different projects and help them divide the work into steps. Hover a bit, under the guise of filling up the soda and champagne glasses, just to make sure things are going in the right direction. Step in to help whenever anyone feels overwhelmed, and make sure people feel comfortable taking breaks (this is a party, not work). It's easy if everyone helps with the first step, then as things are ready for the next steps, some people move on while others keep making the foundation pieces. The small groups will make for some great conversations and the finished projects will stack up quickly.

6. If the projects don't all get done, that's okay. Try to get most of them to a point where you could manageably finish them. You got a great head start, at least, and you should be able to finish them off. If not, throw another party! As if you needed an excuse. ✳

Templates

*Blossoming Thanks template
page 28*

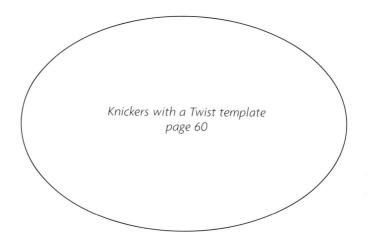

*Knickers with a Twist template
page 60*

*Guest Survival Kit
page 54*

Maybe, Baby! template, page 64, enlarge to 105%

Sticky Guest Book template, page 114, enlarge to 125%

Guests

[paste photo here]

[paste photo here]

wishes for the couple:

wishes for the couple:

Resources

CRAFT SUPPLIES

A.C. Moore
www.acmoore.com

JoAnn Fabrics
www.joann.com

Michaels
www.michaels.com

Pearl
www.pearlpaint.com

BASIC BUILDING SUPPLIES

Home Depot
www.homedepot.com

Lowe's
www.lowes.com

SPECIALTY PAPER AND SUPPLIES

Kate's Paperie
561 Broadway
New York, NY 10012
(888) 941-9169
www.katespaperie.com
The landmark store is available not just to those wandering through SOHO—there are also locations in Greenwich Village, the Upper East Side, and (most importantly) online. Now you can order the exotic papers, journals, and paper accessories online or over the phone.

Paper Source
www.paper-source.com
Locations include Chicago, Cambridge, Minneapolis, and Kansas City (check the Web site for other cities). Here you'll find papers of all kinds, both luxurious and simple. You'll also find adhesives, book-binding materials, decorations, and other high-quality goods.

SPECIALTY STORES AND RESOURCES

Black Ink
5 Brattle St., Harvard Sq.,
Cambridge, MA 02138
(617) 497-1221
and
101 Charles St.,
Boston, MA 02114
(617) 723-3883

Black Ink Home
370 Broadway,
Cambridge, MA 02139
(617) 576-0707
Black Ink, and its spinoff of larger goods, ceramics, and furniture called Black Ink Home, are a treasure trove of inspiring and useful items. From "sushi-pops" to lunch boxes and bowling-ball patches, the genius behind these stores collects the best of what's out there—kitch, industrial, and elegant—for the customers who outfit their homes and projects with their goodies.

Bead Works
23 Church St.
Cambridge, MA 02138
(617) 868-9777
and
1076 Boylston St.
Boston, MA 02215
(617) 247-7227
www.beadworksboston.com

Charles Ro Supply Co.
662 Cross St.
Malden, MA 02148
(781) 321-0090
www.charlesro.com

eBay
www.ebay.com
Want toys, vases, vintage
girl scout patches, or anything
else you can't seem to find in
stores? Check eBay.

HobbyCraft
(stores throughout the UK)
Head Office
Bournemouth
United Kingdom
44 1202 596 100

John Lewis
(stores throughout the UK)
Flagship Store
Oxford.
London W1A 1EX
United Kingdom
44 20 7269 7711

Mariage Freres
70 avenue des Terroirs
de France
75012 Paris
FRANCE
www.mariagefreres.com
01 43 47 18 54
Fax : 01 43 46 60 60
Unbelievable teas from the
oldest French importer of teas
(their history goes back to
the 1660s). Superb blends and
styles make a great addition
to a gift, a nice selection for a
get-together, or a soothing
moment to yourself. Try
Vanille des Îles.

Tender Buttons
143 E. 62nd St.
New York, NY 10021
(212) 758-7004
A tiny store can hold quite a
lot of buttons—from inexpensive replacements for a white
button-down to elaborate and
expensive antiques. If you are
searching for just the right button to add to a project, they
will provide ample choices.
With so many beautiful choices,
you'll end up leaving with
more than you came in for.

The Great Wind-Up
93 Pike St. #201
Seattle, WA 98101
(206) 621-9370
www.greatwindup.com
Wind-up and tin toys.

About the Authors

Laura McFadden, a graphic designer in Somerville, Mass., arrived at her 1991 wedding to Matthew Cogliano in a vintage T-bird (à la Thelma and Louise). Guests danced at a historic house to a cowboy-boot-clad rockabilly band. The 110 guests did not melt in the 100° heat, but the icing on the cake did.

Laura is a former art director for *Inc.* magazine. In 1999, she started Laura McFadden Design, Inc. Her clients have included *Boston Magazine, CFO magazine, Harvard Medical Alumni Bulletin*, the Harvard Aids Institute, Pohly and Partners, Rockport Publishers, and Commonwealth Editions. She has been a contributing writer/craftsperson for various magazines and books.

April Paffrath, a writer and editor in Cambridge, Mass., wore a burgundy dress to her 2001 wedding to Matthew Krom. They walked to the church together—and stopped in a shoe store on the way. April and Matt—and nearly all the 26 guests—took the subway downtown to celebrate with a six-hour dinner party. Unable to choose between French or Italian stationery, they sent invitations by e-mail.

April's work has appeared in publications such as *Martha Stewart Living, Cape Cod Life,* and *Natural Home.* She has edited both books and magazines, including a Harvard Business School Press *HBR* series and *Technology Review.* She is the former managing editor of *Scientific American Explorations.*

Acknowledgments

We'd like to thank Silke Braun, Regina Grenier, Mary Ann Hall, Kristy Mulkern, Winnie Prentiss, and all the other great people at Rockport Publishers who made this book possible.

Special thanks to Paul DiMattia, Carolynn DeCillo, Jean Marie Fiocchi-Marden, Timothy Marden, Joseph and Cecilia McFadden, Jimmy Merrill, Alison Mirman, Carol Lieb, Isabelle Malouf, and Eric Parkes.

Thanks also to our friends and cohorts who continually encourage us, inspire our creativity, and serve as sounding boards for all our wild ideas.

DEDICATION

To Matthew, my husband and best friend, whose kindness and support is an everyday inspiration to me. –LM

To the one with the stunning sense of humor, sweetness, and style: my husband, Matthew. –AP